2016 SPRING COLLECTION

BY KNIT PICKS

Photography by Amy Cave
Shot on location at Cistus Nursery in Portland, Oregon www.cistus.com

Printed in the United States of America

First Printing, 2016

ISBN 978-1-62767-116-3

Versa Press, Inc
800-447-7829

www.versapress.com

CONTENTS

Where earth and air meet, there is ground fresh with the changing seasons. The Knit Picks 2016 spring collection, *Aura*, celebrates this transition with light garments and accessories perfect for layering. From the Solana Cardigan, pictured on the cover, featuring both easy lace and delicate cables, to Rie, an ethereal layer that adds drama to any ensemble, to the show-stopping Chanteuse Dress, these are garments that will take you from cooler days to warmer weather. If accessories are your delight, the Vita Cowl, in baby-soft Alpaca Cloud lace yarn, will have you feeling adorned in a cloud indeed, while Catamaran will leave you feeling both grounded and light in stripes and eyelets. From a lacy shawl to a button-back shirt, there's something for everyone in *Aura*, a collection you'll knit from for many warm seasons to come.

SOLANA CARDIGAN

by Irina Anikeeva

FINISHED MEASUREMENTS

31 (35, 38, 40, 44, 48)" /78.5 (89, 96.5, 101.5, 112, 122) cm bust circumference (with fronts overlapping to approximate back width). Garment is meant to be worn with 1-2"/2.5-5 cm of positive ease.

YARN

Knit Picks Comfy Sport (75% Pima Cotton, 25% Acrylic; 136 yards/50g): Ivory 24429, 8 (8, 9, 9, 10, 11) skeins.

NEEDLES

US 5 (3.75mm) straight and 32" or longer circular needles plus DPN's, or size to obtain gauge
US 3 (3.25mm) 32" or longer circular needles plus DPN's, or size to obtain gauge

NOTIONS

Yarn Needle
Stitch Markers
Scrap Yarn or 2 Stitch Holders
Safety Pins or Removable Markers
Cable Needle

GAUGE:

27 sts and 29 rows = 4" in Lattice pattern on size larger needle, blocked.
17 sts and 32 rows = 4" in Mesh pattern on size larger needle, blocked.
26 sts and 30 rows = 4" in 1×1 Rib on smaller needle, blocked.

Solana Cardigan

Notes:

Solana's airy mesh fabric and drape-front design make it a must-have layering piece for spring and summer days and, of course, nights.

This cardigan features a unique top-down seamless construction: the saddle yoke with a clean lattice pattern on a purl ground is worked first, from side to side, then stitches for the body are picked up along back and right and left front pieces. They are worked separately back and forth in mesh pattern, then joined and the lower body is worked in one piece to the lower edge. Stitches for the sleeves are picked up around the armhole and the sleeves are worked from top down in the round.

Circular needle is used to accommodate the large number of stitches.

The chart is read on RS rows (odd numbers) from right to left, and WS rows (even numbers) from left to right.

Mesh Pattern (worked flat over an even number of sts)
Row 1(RS): *YO, SSK; rep from * to the end of row.
Row 2 (WS): Purl all sts.
Row 3: *SSK, YO; rep from * to the end of row.
Row 4: Purl all sts.
Repeat Rows 1-4 for pattern.

Mesh Pattern (in the round over an even number of sts)
Row 1(RS): *YO, SSK; rep from * to the end of row.
Row 2 (WS): K all sts.
Row 3: *SSK, YO; rep from * to the end of row.
Row 4: K all sts.
Repeat Rows 1-4 for pattern.

Make 1 Stitch (M1): With LH needle tip, pick up the thread between sts from front to back. K lifted loop TBL.

Make 1 Purl Stitch (M1P): With LH needle tip, pick up the thread between sts from front to back. P lifted loop TBL.

Backwards-Loop Cast-On Method
Place the working yarn over your thumb. The RH needle goes under the yarn at the base of your thumb and over the yarn at the top of your thumb. Tighten your newly cast on st.

Tubular Bind-off method
Cut the yarn, leaving a tail about 3 times the circumference of the knitting to be bound off, and thread the tail onto a yarn needle.
Step 1: Working from right to left, insert the yarn needle P-wise (from right to left) through the first K st and pull the yarn through.
Step 2: Bring the yarn needle behind the K st, then insert it K-wise (from left to right) into the second st (this will be a P st) and pull the yarn through.
Step 3: Insert the yarn needle into the first K st K-wise and slip this st off the knitting needle.
Step 4: Skip the first P st, insert the yarn needle P-wise into the next K st, and pull the yarn through.

Step 5: Insert the yarn needle into the first P st P-wise and slip this st off the knitting needle.
Step 6: Bring the yarn needle behind the K st, then insert it K-wise into the second st (this will be a P st), and pull the yarn through. Repeat Steps 3-6 until 1 st remains on the knitting needle. Insert the yarn needle P-wise through this last st, draw the yarn through, and pull tight to secure.

DIRECTIONS

Saddle
With larger straight needles CO 44 (44, 44, 52, 52, 52) sts.
Next Row (WS): P all sts.
Work Rows 15-16 (13-16, 11-16, 15-16, 15-16, 11-16) of Lattice Chart. You will work sts 1-10 of chart, then work 8-st chart repetition 3 (3, 3, 4, 4, 4) times, ending with sts 19-28.
Work Rows 1-16 of chart 1 (1, 1, 2, 2, 2) times.
Work Rows 1-9 (1-11, 1-11, 1-3, 1-9, 1-7) of chart.

Shape Neck
Next Row (WS): At the beginning of row BO 21 (21, 21, 25, 25, 25) sts, work in pattern to end of row. BO 1 st at beginning of next 2 WS rows. 21 (21, 21, 25, 25, 25) sts.
Work Rows 15-16 (0, 0, 9-16, 15-16, 13-16) of chart.
Work Rows 1-16 of chart 2 (3, 3, 2, 3, 3) times.
Work Rows 1-2 (0, 0, 1-8, 1-4, 1-6) of chart.
Note: Do not cross the cables if you don't have enough sts.
Using Backwards-Loop Cast-On Method, CO 1 st at the end of next 2 RS rows, then at the end of next RS row CO 21 (21, 21, 25, 25, 25) sts. 44 (44, 44, 52, 52, 52) sts.
Work Rows 8-16 (6-16, 6-16, 14-16, 10-16, 12-16) of chart.
Work Rows 1-16 of chart 1 (1, 1, 2, 2, 2) times.
Work Rows 1-3 (1-5, 1-7, 1-3, 1-3, 1-7) of chart.
Next Row (WS): P all sts.

BO all sts.

Block saddle to schematic measurements.

Back
With RS facing, mark center of back edge of saddle and place 2 safety pins; first 1" to the right and second 1" to the left of the center marker. Remove center marker.
With RS facing, beginning at right end, with larger circular needle PU and K 28 (34, 34, 38, 42, 44) sts along back edge of saddle to first pin, PU and K 11 sts between pins, PU and K 28 (34, 34, 38, 42, 44) sts along back edge to end of saddle. 67 (79, 79, 87, 95, 99) sts are picked up for the back. Remove safety pins.
Next Row (WS): Purl all sts.
Next Row (RS): K2, PM, work Row 1 of Mesh Pattern Chart over 26 (32, 32, 36, 40, 42) sts, PM, (K1, P1) 5 times, K1, PM, work in Mesh Pattern to 2 sts before end, K2.
Next Row (WS): P2, SM, work Row 2 of Mesh Pattern Chart to M, SM, P1, (K1, P1) 5 times, SM, work in Mesh Pattern to 2 sts before end of row, SM, P2.
Cont to work in pattern as established, working Rows 3-4 of Mesh Pattern, then repeating Rows 1-4 of Mesh Pattern, until piece measures 4.25 (4.25, 5, 5.25, 5.25, 5.75)" from beginning of Mesh Pattern, ending with WS row.
Break yarn, place all sts on holder. Take note of last row number.

Right Front

With bigger circular needle and RS facing, beginning at right end of saddle, PU and K 18 (20, 22, 24, 26, 28) sts between first st and beginning of BO sts.

Row 1 (WS): P all sts.

Row 2 (RS): K2, PM, work Row 1 of Mesh Pattern to end; using Backwards-Loop Method, CO 2 sts. 20 (22, 24, 26, 28, 30) sts.

Row 3: Work Row 2 of Mesh Pattern to 2 sts before end, SM, P2.

Row 4: K2, SM, work in Mesh Pattern 16 (18, 20, 22, 24, 26) sts, K2, CO 2 sts. 22 (24, 26, 28, 30, 32) sts.

Row 5: P all sts.

Row 6: K2, SM, work in Mesh Pattern 18 (20, 22, 24, 26, 28) sts, K2, CO 31 (33, 37, 35, 37, 39) sts. 53 (57, 63, 63, 67, 71) sts.

Row 7: P all sts.

Row 8: K2, SM, work in Mesh Pattern 20 (22, 24, 26, 28, 30) sts, K22 (24, 28, 26, 28, 30) sts, PM, (P1, K1) 4 times, K1.

Row 9: Sl 1 P-wise, (P1, K1) 4 times, SM, P to end.

Row 10: K2, SM, work next row of Mesh Pattern to M, SM, (P1, K1) 4 times, K1.

Row 11: Sl 1 P-wise, (P1, K1) 4 times, SM, P to end.

Work all sts even as established until piece measures 4.25 (4.25, 5, 5.25, 5.25, 5.25)" from beginning of Mesh Pattern, ending with WS row, making sure to end up with same row of Mesh Pattern as Back.

Break yarn, place all sts on holder.

Left Front

With larger circular needle and RS facing, beginning at left neck opening after BO sts, PU and K 18 (20, 22, 24, 26, 28) sts along selvage edge of saddle.

Row 1 (WS): P to end; using Backwards-Loop Method CO 2 sts at the end of row. 20 (22, 24, 26, 28, 30) sts.

Row 2 (RS): K2, work Row 1 of Mesh Pattern to last 2 sts, PM, K2.

Row 3 : P to end, CO 2 sts. 22 (24, 26, 28, 30, 32) sts.

Row 4: K2, work next row of Mesh Pattern to M, SM, K2.

Row 5: P to end, CO 31 (33, 37, 35, 37, 39) sts. 53 (57, 63, 63, 67, 71) sts.

Row 6: K31 (33, 37, 35, 37, 39), work next row of Mesh Pattern to M, SM, K2.

Row 7: P to 9 sts before end, PM, (K1, P1) 4 times, P1.

Row 8: Sl 1 K-wise, (K1, P1) 4 times, work next row of Mesh Pattern to 2 sts before end, K2.

Work all sts even as established until piece measures 4.25 (4.25, 5, 5.25, 5.25, 5.25)" from beginning of Mesh Pattern, ending with WS row, making sure to end up with same row of Mesh Pattern as Back and Right Front.

Join Fronts and Back

Next Row (RS): Sl 1 K-wise, (K1, P1) 4 times, SM, work next row of Mesh Pattern, removing M, over 44 (48, 54, 54, 58, 62) sts, PM, using Backwards-Loop Method, CO 9 sts for underarm, PM, work in Mesh Pattern over 28 (34, 34, 38, 42, 44) held back sts, SM, (K1, P1) 5 times, K1, SM, work in Mesh Pattern over 28 (34, 34, 38, 42, 44) held back sts, PM, CO 9 sts for underarm, PM, work in Mesh Pattern, removing M, over 44 (48, 54, 54, 58, 62) held right front sts, SM, (P1, K1) 4 times, K1. 191 (211, 223, 231, 247, 259) sts.

Work 1 WS row in pattern as established, P underarm sts.

Lower Body

Next Row (RS): Sl 1 K-wise, (K1, P1) 4 times, SM, work next row of Mesh Pattern to M, SM, (K1, P1) 2 times, place safety pin for center of armhole, (K1, P1) 2 times, K1, SM, work back sts to underarm M as established, SM, K1, (P1, K1) 2 times, place safety pin for center of armhole, (P1, K1) 2 times, SM, work right front sts as established.

Work even until piece measures 14.5 (14.5, 14.5, 15, 15, 15.5)" from armhole, ending with WS row.

Rib Set-Up Row (RS): Sl 1, (K1, P10) 4 times, SM, K to M, SM, (K1, P1) 4 times, K1, SM, K to M, (K1, P1) 5 times, K1, SM, K to M, K1, (P1, K1) 4 times, SM, K to M, (P1, K1) 4 times, K1.

Rib

Change to smaller circular needles.

Size 31" Only:

Inc Row (WS): Sl 1, (P1, K1) 4 times, SM, P2, (P1, M1P, P1) 20 times, P2, SM, (P1, K1) 4 times, P1, SM, P1, (P1, M1P, P1) 13 times, P1, SM, P1, (K1, P1) 5 times, SM, P1, (P1, M1P, P1) 13 times, P1, SM, P1, (K1, P1) 4 times, SM, P2, (P1, M1P, P1) 20 times, P2, SM, (K1, P1) 4 times, P1. 257 sts.

Size 35" Only:

Inc Row (WS): Sl 1, (P1, K1) 4 times, SM, P2, (P1, M1P, P1) 22 times, P2, SM, (P1, K1) 4 times, P1, SM, P2, (P1, M1P, P1) 15 times, P2, SM, P1, (K1, P1) 5 times, SM, P2, (P1, M1P, P1) 15 times, P2, SM, P1, (K1, P1) 4 times, SM, P2, (P1, M1P, P1) 22 times, P2, SM, (K1, P1) 4 times, P1. 285 sts.

Size 38" Only:

Inc Row (WS): Sl 1, (P1, K1) 4 times, SM, P1, (P1, M1P, P1) 26 times, P1, SM, (P1, K1) 4 times, P1, SM, (P1, M1P, P1) 17 times, SM, P1, (K1, P1) 5 times, SM, (P1, M1P, P1) 17 times, SM, P1, (K1, P1) 4 times, SM, P1, (P1, M1P, P1) 26 times, P1, SM, (K1, P1) 4 times, P1. 309 sts.

Size 40" Only:

Inc Row (WS): Sl 1, (P1, K1) 4 times, SM, P1, (P1, M1P, P1) 26 times, P1, SM, (P1, K1) 4 times, P1, SM, P2, (P1, M1P, P1) 17 times, P2, SM, P1, (K1, P1) 5 times, SM, P2, (P1, M1P, P1) 17 times, P2, SM, P1, (K1, P1) 4 times, SM, P1, (P1, M1P, P1) 26 times, P1, SM, (K1, P1) 4 times, P1. 317 sts.

Size 44" Only:

Inc Row (WS): Sl 1, (P1, K1) 4 times, SM, P3, (P1, M1P, P1) 26 times, P3, SM, (P1, K1) 4 times, P1, SM, (P1, M1P, P1) 21 times, SM, P1, (K1, P1) 5 times, SM, (P1, M1P, P1) 21 times, SM, P1, (K1, P1) 4 times, SM, P3, (P1, M1P, P1) 26 times, P3, SM, (K1, P1) 4 times, P1. 341 sts.

Size 48" Only:

Inc Row (WS): Sl 1, (P1, K1) 4 times, SM, P3, (P1, M1P, P1) 28 times, P3, SM, (P1, K1) 4 times, P1, SM, (M1P, P1) 3 times, (M1P, P2) 19 times, (M1P, P1) 3 times, SM, P1, (K1, P1) 5 times, SM, (M1P, P1) 3 times, (M1P, P2) 19 times, (M1P, P1) 3 times, SM, P1, (K1, P1) 4 times, SM, P3, (P1, M1P, P1) 28 times, P3, SM, (K1, P1) 4 times, P1. 365 sts.

All Sizes:

Next Row (RS): Removing markers as you go, Sl 1 st K-wise, (K1, P1) to 2 sts before end, K2.

Next Row (WS): Sl 1 P-wise, P1, (K1, P1) to 1 st before end, P1.

Cont working in 1×1 Rib as established for another 12 rows.

BO all sts in pattern.

Right Sleeve

With larger DPNs and RS facing, beginning at marked center of underarm, PU and K 5 sts along underarm, 58 (62, 64, 66, 68, 70) sts evenly around armhole, ending 4 sts before center of underarm, PU and K 4 sts along underarm. 67 (71, 73, 75, 77, 79) sts total. PM for beginning of rnd and join in the rnd.

Next Rnd: (K1, P1) 2 times, PM, K1, work Row 1 of Mesh pattern in rnd over 58 (62, 64, 66, 68, 70) sts, K1, PM, P1, K1, P1.

Next Rnd: (K1, P1) 2 times, SM, K1, work Row 2 of Mesh pattern in rnd to 1 st before M, K1, SM, P1, K1, P1.

Working marked section and K sts outside markers in established rib, work remaining sts in Mesh Pattern even for 2 more rnds.

Dec Rnd: Work 4 rib sts, SM, SSK, work in pattern to 2 sts before next M, K2tog, SM, work 3 rib sts. 2 sts dec.

Next Rnd: Work 4 rib sts, SM, K1, work in pattern to 1 st before next M, K1, SM, work 3 rib sts.

Note: when shaping sleeves, make sure to keep the mesh pattern and number of sts after each Dec Rnd correct. Each YO should have a corresponding decrease, so you may have to work a K st rather than SSK in some rows to keep st count correct.

Repeat Dec Rnd 11 (12, 13, 12, 13, 13) more times every 6 (5, 5, 6, 5, 6)th rnd. 43 (45, 45, 49, 49, 51) sts.

Continue to work as established until sleeve measures 11 (11, 11, 11.5, 11.5, 11.5)", or desired length.

Next Rnd: (K1, P1) 2 times, SM, K to M, SM, P1, K1, P1.

Change to smaller DPNs.

Size 31" Only:

Inc Rnd: (K1, P1) 2 times, SM, K2, (M1, K4) 8 times, M1, K2, SM, P1, K1, P1. 52 sts.

Sizes 35" and 38" Only:

Inc Rnd: (K1, P1) 2 times, SM, K2, (M1, K3) 3 times, (M1, K4) 4 times, (M1, K3) 3 times, M1, K2, SM, P1, K1, P1. 56 sts.

Sizes 40" and 44" Only:

Inc Rnd: (K1, P1) 2 times, SM, K2, M1, K3, (M1, K4) 8 times, M1, K3, M1, K2, SM, P1, K1, P1. 60 sts.

Size 48" Only:

Inc Rnd: (K1, P1) 2 times, SM, K1, (M1, K3) 14 times, M1, K1, SM, P1, K1, P1. 66 sts.

All Sizes:

Next Rnd: (K1, P1) to end of rnd, removing all markers except beginning of rnd as you go. Cont to work in 1×1 Rib for a total of 1".

BO all sts, using Tubular Bind-Off Method.

Left Sleeve

With larger DPNs and RS facing, beginning at marked center of underarm, PU and K 4 sts along underarm, 58 (62, 64, 66, 68, 70) sts evenly around armhole, ending 5 sts before center of underarm,
PU and K 5 sts along underarm. 67 (71, 73, 75, 77, 79) sts. PM for beginning of rnd and join in the rnd.

Next Rnd: P1, K1, P1, PM, K1, work Row 1 of Mesh Pattern in rnd over 58 (62, 64, 66, 68, 70) sts, K1, PM, (P1, K1) twice.

Next Rnd: P1, K1, P1, SM, K1, work Row 2 of Mesh Pattern in rnd to 1 st before M, K1, SM, (P1, K1) twice.

Working marked section and K sts outside markers in established rib, work remaining sts in Mesh Pattern even for 2 more rnds.

Dec Rnd: Work 3 rib sts, SM, SSK, work in pattern to 2 sts before next M, K2tog, SM, work 4 rib sts. 2 sts dec.

Repeat Dec Rnd 11 (12, 13, 12, 13, 13) more times, every 6 (5, 5, 6, 5, 6)th rnd. 43 (45, 45, 49, 49, 51) sts.

Continue to work even until sleeve measures 11 (11, 11.5, 11.5, 11.5)" or desired length.

Next Rnd: P1, K1, P1, SM, K to M, SM, (P1, K1) 2 times.

Change to smaller DPNs.

Size 31" Only:

Inc Rnd: P1, K1, P1, SM, K2, (M1, K4) 8 times, M1, K2, SM, (P1, K1) twice. 52 sts.

Sizes 35" and 38" Only:

Inc Rnd: P1, K1, P1, SM, K2, (M1, K3) 3 times, (M1, K4) 4 times, (M1, K3) 3 times, M1, K2, SM, (P1, K1) twice. 56 sts.

Sizes 40" and 44" Only:

Inc Rnd: P1, K1, K2, M1, K3, (M1, K4) 8 times, M1, K3, M1, K2, SM, (P1, K1) twice. 60 sts.

Size 48" Only:

Inc Rnd: P1, K1, SM, K1, (M1, K3) 14 times, M1, K1, SM, (P1, K1) twice. 66 sts.

All Sizes:

Next Rnd: (P1, K1) to end of rnd. Cont to work in 1×1 Rib for a total of 1".

BO all sts, using Tubular Bind-Off Method.

Finishing

Neckband

With RS facing and smaller circular needle, PU and K 153 (173, 173, 179, 189, 195) sts evenly spaced around neck opening, including front bands.

Next Row (WS): Sl 1 P-wise, P1, (K1, P1) to last 1 st, P1.

Next Row (RS): Sl 1 K-wise, (K1, P1) to last 2 sts, K2.

Work in 1×1 Rib as established for 7 more rows.

BO all sts, using Tubular Bind-Off Method.

Weave in ends, block to measurements.

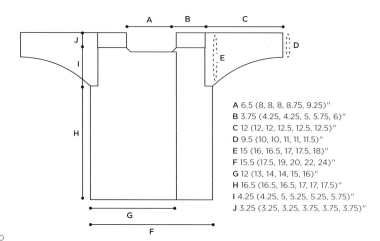

A 6.5 (8, 8, 8, 8.75, 9.25)"
B 3.75 (4.25, 4.25, 5, 5.75, 6)"
C 12 (12, 12, 12.5, 12.5, 12.5)"
D 9.5 (10, 10, 11, 11, 11.5)"
E 15 (16, 16.5, 17, 17.5, 18)"
F 15.5 (17.5, 19, 20, 22, 24)"
G 12 (13, 14, 14, 15, 16)"
H 16.5 (16.5, 16.5, 17, 17, 17.5)"
I 4.25 (4.25, 5, 5.25, 5.25, 5.75)"
J 3.25 (3.25, 3.25, 3.75, 3.75, 3.75)"

Solana Chart

Column numbers (top, left to right): 28 27 26 25 24 23 22 21 20 19 18 17 16 15 14 13 12 11 10 9 8 7 6 5 4 3 2 1

Row numbers (left): 16, 14, 12, 10, 8, 6, 4, 2
Row numbers (right): 15, 13, 11, 9, 7, 5, 3, 1

Legend

knit
RS: knit stitch
WS: purl stitch

purl
RS: purl stitch
WS: knit stitch

C1 over 1 left
sl 1 to CN, hold in back, k1, k1 from CN

C1 over 1 right P
sl 1 to CN, hold in back. k1, p1 from CN

C1 over 1 left P
sl 1 to CN, hold in front. p1, k1 from CN

C1 over 1 right
sl1 to CN, hold in front. k1, k1 from CN

pattern repeat

RIE

by Cristina T. Ghirlanda

FINISHED MEASUREMENTS

51.5 (52, 54.5, 58.5, 62.5, 67.5, 71.5)" finished bust measurement; garment is meant to be worn with 14-18" of positive ease.

YARN

Knit Picks Aloft (75% Super Kid Mohair, 25% Silk; 246 yards/25g):
Silver 25214, 2 (2, 2, 2, 2, 2, 3) balls.

NEEDLES

US 10.5 (6.5mm) circular needle of length at least 40", or size to obtain gauge
US 8 (5mm) DPNs or circular needle, or three sizes smaller than needle to obtain gauge, for armhole band and hem.

NOTIONS

Yarn Needle
Scrap Yarn or Stitch Holder
Stitch Markers

GAUGE

12 sts and 18 rows = 4" in St st worked flat or in the round on larger needle, blocked.
12 sts and 26 rows = 4" in 1x1 Rib in the round on smaller needle, blocked.

Rie

Notes:

This sweater is worked from the bottom up in the round to the armholes, then the front and back are worked separately and joined at the shoulder.

Cable Cast-on

Make a slip knot and place it on the left needle. K into this st. Insert left needle tip into this loop from right to left. *Insert the tip of the right needle between the two sts on the left needle. Wrap the yarn around and draw a loop through. Insert the left needle tip into this loop from right to left and remove the right needle from the st. Repeat from * until the required number of sts are on the needle, lightly tightening the sts as you go along.

Elastic Bind-off

Following the 1x1 Rib pattern, work 1 st, *YO, work 1 st, pass the rightmost 2 sts on right needle over the last worked st; repeat from * to end.

1x1 Rib (worked in the rnd over an even number of sts)

All Rnds: *K1, P1; rep from * to end of rnd.

DIRECTIONS

Body

With smaller needle, use the Cable Cast-on method to loosely CO 154 (156, 164, 176, 188, 202, 214) sts.
PM, join and begin working in the round, being careful not to twist sts.

Work in 1x1 Rib until ribbing measures 1".
Change to larger needle.
Work even in St st (K all rnds) until piece measures 8.75 (8.75, 8.5, 8.75, 9, 9.5, 10.25)" from CO.

Divide for Front and Back

BO 0 (0, 2, 6, 9, 14, 17) underarm sts, knit until you have 77 (78, 80, 82, 85, 87, 90) sts for Front, BO 0 (0, 2, 6, 9, 14, 17) underarm sts, knit remaining sts for Back. Do not cut yarn, and continue to work back and forth for Back. 77 (78, 80, 82, 85, 87, 90) sts for Front and Back.

Back

Work even in St st (K on RS, P on WS) until armhole measures 6.75 (7.25, 7.75, 8, 8, 8, 8)", ending with a WS row.
Loosely BO all sts. Cut yarn and leave long tail for shoulder seam.

Front

With WS facing, join yarn at the right underarm, work as for Back.

Finishing

With RS of Back facing RS of Front, along the BO edge seam the outer 6.75 (7, 7.25, 7.25, 7.5, 7.75, 8)" of both ends for shoulders, working from the armhole edge towards neck opening.

Armhole Band

With smaller needle, starting at the center of the underarm, PU 1 st for every BO st (no stitch to PU for the smallest 2 sizes), then PU 2 sts every 3 rows until the BO sts, PU 1 st for every BO st (no stitch to PU for the smallest 2 sizes), making sure that you have an even number of sts.
Work in 1x1 Rib until ribbing measures 0.5".
Use the Elastic Bind-off method to BO all sts in patt. Cut yarn. Repeat for the other armhole.

Weave in ends, wash and block if desired. Note: Sizes other than the smallest 2 sizes have additional underarm sts and hence do not block to a rectangle as shown. Block area above armhole to Back Width and area below armhole to Bottom Width.

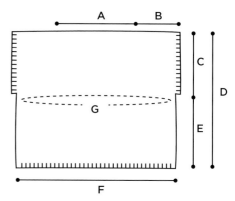

A 12.25 (12.25, 12.5, 13, 13.5, 13.5, 14)"
B 6.75 (7, 7.25, 7.25, 7.5, 7.75, 8)"
C 6.75 (7.25, 7.75, 8, 8, 8, 8)"
D 15.5 (16, 16.25, 16.75, 17, 17.5, 18.25)"
E 8.75 (8.75, 8.5, 8.75, 9, 9.5, 10.25)"
F 25.75 (26, 27.25, 29.25, 31.25, 33.75, 35.75)"
G 51.5 (52, 54.5, 58.5, 62.5, 67.5, 71.5)"

POETIC SKIRT

by Katy Banks

FINISHED MEASUREMENTS

28 (30, 32, 34, 36, 38, 40, 42, 44)"
finished waist, unstretched, to be worn 2"
below natural waist with zero ease.

YARN

Knit Picks Alpaca Cloud Lace (100% Baby
Alpaca; 440 yards/50g): Emma 26790, 8
(8, 8, 8, 8, 8, 9, 9, 9) hanks.

NEEDLES

US 2.5 (3mm) 32" or longer circular
needle, or size to obtain gauge
Smaller sizes will also need a 24" circular
needle of the same size

NOTIONS

Yarn Needle
Stitch Marker
2" wide non-rolling elastic 1" longer than
finished waist
Sewing needle and thread for sewing
elastic ends together

GAUGE

26 sts and 40 rnds = 4" in St st in the
round with yarn held doubled, blocked.
26 sts and 38 rnds = 4" in St st in the
round with single strand of yarn, blocked.

Poetic Skirt

Notes:

This pull-on skirt is worked from the top down in the round and increases are worked around the complete circumference so the skirt has no front or back. You will begin with the yarn held doubled to create the modest upper skirt, then work with a single strand for the sheer lower skirt. The hem is worked with doubled yarn to provide visual and physical weight.

2x2 Rib (worked in the round over a multiple of 4 sts):
Every Round: *K2, P2 rep from * to the end of the rnd.

Garter Stitch (in the round):
Round 1: K.
Round 2: P.
Repeat Rnds 1-2 for pattern.

DIRECTIONS
Waist

With two strands of yarn held together and using the elastic method of your choice, CO 208 (224, 240, 256, 272, 284, 300, 316, 328) sts. Join for working in the rnd, being careful to not twist the sts. PM for beginning/end rnd.
Work 2x2 Rib for 2.25".
P one rnd (turning round).
Work 2x2 Rib for 2.25" more.

Skirt

Continue working with two strands of yarn held together as though they were one. When the skirt measures 22.5" from the turning round, break one strand of yarn and continue with a single strand.
AT THE SAME TIME change to St st (K every st, every rnd) and work 9 rnds even. Work increases as follows:
Increase Rnd A: *K 18 (22, 24, 28, 30, 35, 37, 45, 46) sts, M1, PM, rep from * to end of rnd, ending with K 10 (4, 0, 4, 2, 4, 4, 1, 6). 219 (234, 250, 265, 281, 292, 308, 323, 335) sts.
Work 9 rnds even.
Increase Rnd B: *K to M, M1, SM, rep from * to end of rnd, do not M1 at the end of the rnd. 11 (10, 10, 9, 9, 8, 8, 7, 7) sts inc.
Rep the last 10 rnds 12 (24, 9, 21, 6, 18, 3, 15, 0) times more. 362 (484, 350, 463, 344, 444, 340, 435, 342) sts on needle.
In the next rnd, remove each M as you come to it, except the beginning/end rnd M. Work 9 rnds even.

Increase Rnd C: * K 36 (53, 38, 57, 43, 63, 48, 72, 57) sts, M1, PM, rep from * to end of rnd, ending with K 2 (7, 8, 7, 0, 3, 4, 3, 0). 10 (9, 9, 8, 8, 7, 7, 6, 6) sts inc.
All sizes except size 30: Work 9 rnds even. Work Increase Rnd C again. Rep the last 10 rnds 11 (-, 14, 2, 17, 5, 20, 8, 23) times more. 492 (493, 494, 495, 496, 493, 494, 495, 492) sts on needle. Continue to work even with a single strand of yarn until skirt measures 34" from turning rnd.

Hem

Continue for all sizes. Join a second ball of yarn and continue working with two strands of yarn held together as though they were one. Work Garter Stitch for 4". BO loosely.

Finishing

Weave in ends, wash and block to diagram. With sewing needle and thread, sew elastic into a circle, overlapping the ends 1". Place elastic inside waist band (WS), between the purled turning rnd and St st section. Fold waist band facing along the turning rnd to the inside of the skirt, enclosing elastic. Using yarn needle and two strands of yarn held together, invisibly sew facing in place.

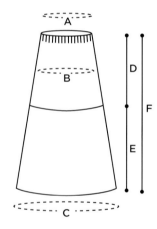

A 28 (30, 32, 34, 36, 38, 40, 42, 44)"
B 41 (43, 45, 47, 49, 51, 53, 55, 57)"
C 76"
D 22.5"
E 15.5"
F 38"

TRELLIS VINES STOLE/PONCHO

by Michele Lee Bernstein

FINISHED MEASUREMENTS

62x18" stole, or folded in half and seamed with ribbon for 31x18" poncho

YARN

Knit Picks Galileo (50% Merino Wool, 50% Viscose from Bamboo; 131 yards/50g): Urchin 26575, 7 balls.

NEEDLES

US 5 (3.75mm) straight or circular needles, or size to obtain gauge

NOTIONS

Yarn Needle
Stitch Markers
Scrap Yarn or Stitch Holder
4 yards 3/8" Ribbon for seaming poncho, optional

GAUGE

18 sts and 30 rows = 4" in Trellis Vines pattern, blocked. (Gauge for this project is approximate)

Trellis Vines Stole/Poncho

Notes:

The Trellis Vines Stole/Poncho is worked in two identical pieces so that all leaves twine from the scalloped hems up to the shoulder. The pieces are seamed together at the neck/shoulder with a Three Needle Bind Off. The piece can be worn as a stole, or folded in half and laced with ribbon to create a poncho.

The chart is followed from right to left on RS (odd numbered) rows, and left to right on WS (even numbered) rows.

Three Needle Bind Off

Hold both pieces of work together, with right sides facing. Using the remaining yarn from the second piece, insert needle into first st on each needle and knit them off together. *K one more st from each needle in the same way. Pull first completed st from right needle over the second one; one st bound off. Repeat from * until one st remains on right needle. Pull yarn through st to fasten off.

DIRECTIONS

Loosely CO 91 sts using long tail cast on. K 2 rows. Begin working Trellis Vines pattern from Trellis Vines Chart or written instructions. Sts 6-21 of chart repeat 5 times across row. Work Rows 1-32 of Trellis Vines pattern 7 times.

Trellis Vines Pattern (worked flat over multiple of 16 sts plus 11)

Row 1 (RS): K2, YO, K2tog, K1, PM, *P1, (SSK, YO) 3x, K1, P1, YO, K2, SSK, K3, PM; rep from * 4 more times, P1, K1, SSK, YO, K2. Slip markers on subsequent rows.

Row 2 and all even rows through 32 (WS): K2, P3, K1, (P7, K1, P7, K1) 5x, P3, K2.

Row 3: K2, YO, K2tog, K1, *P1, (SSK, YO) 3x, K1, P1, K1, YO, K2, SSK, K2; rep from * 4 more times, P1, K1, SSK, YO, K2.

Row 5: K2, YO, K2tog, K1, *P1, (SSK, YO) 3x, K1, P1, K2, YO, K2, SSK, K1; rep from * 4 more times, P1, K1, SSK, YO, K2.

Row 7: K2, YO, K2tog, K1, *P1, (SSK, YO) 3x, K1, P1, K3, YO, K2, SSK; rep from * 4 more times, P1, K1, SSK, YO, K2.

Rows 9-16: Rep Rows 1-8.

Row 17: K2, YO, K2tog, K1, *P1, K3, K2tog, K2, YO, P1, K1, (YO, K2tog) 3x; rep from * 4 more times, P1, K1, SSK, YO, K2.

Row 19: K2, YO, K2tog, K1, *P1, K2, K2tog, K2, YO, K1, P1, K1, (YO, K2tog) 3x; rep from * 4 more times, P1, K1, SSK, YO, K2.

Row 21: K2, YO, K2tog, K1, *P1, K1, K2tog, K2, YO, K2, P1, K1, (YO, K2tog) 3x; rep from * 4 more times, P1, K1, SSK, YO, K2.

Row 23: K2, YO, K2tog, K1, *P1, K2tog, K2, YO, K3, P1, K1, (YO, K2tog) 3x; rep from * 4 more times, P1, K1, SSK, YO, K2.

Rows 25-32: Rep Rows 17-24.

Rep Rows 1-32 for pattern.

When 7 repeats (224 rows) of Trellis Vines are complete, place sts on stitch holder or scrap yarn (or use your knitting needle if it's waterproof for blocking, and you have an extra).

CO and work identical second half of stole. When knitting is complete, cut yarn leaving a 2 yard tail (72") that will be used for joining pieces.

Finishing

Wet block both pieces to desired measurements of 20" wide and 32" long, accentuating the wave at the bottom hems. Pieces will bounce back to about 18.5" wide and 31" long. Place pieces with right sides together, and join using Three Needle Bind Off. Sew in all ends. Lightly steam shoulder seam. Stole is complete.

For Poncho, fold Stole in half at shoulder seam. Use ribbon to create a seam in the eyelets along one edge, as you would lace a shoe. Begin at the bottom hem, and work your way up until a 12" opening remains at the neck edge. Tie in a bow, and trim ends as desired.

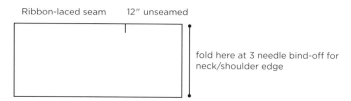

Ribbon-laced seam   12" unseamed

fold here at 3 needle bind-off for neck/shoulder edge

open edge

Trellis Vines Chart

Legend

knit
RS: knit stitch
WS: purl stitch

yo
yarn over

k2tog
Knit two stitches together as one stitch

purl
RS: purl stitch
WS: knit stitch

ssk
Slip one stitch as if to knit, slip another stitch as if to knit. Insert left-hand needle into front of these 2 stitches and knit them together

pattern repeat

MUSE TOP

by Katy Banks

FINISHED MEASUREMENTS

34.5 (38.5, 42.5, 46.5, 50.5, 54.5)" finished bust measurement; garment is meant to be worn with 4" of positive ease.

YARN

Knit Picks Shimmer (70% Baby Alpaca, 30% Silk; 880 yards/100g): Bare 26584, 1 (1, 1, 2, 2, 2) hanks.

NEEDLES

US 3 (3.25mm) straight or circular needles plus same size DPNs and/or two 24" circulars for two-circular technique, or size to obtain gauge.

NOTIONS

Yarn Needle
Stitch Markers
Three 3/8" very lightweight buttons
Sewing Needle
Thread

GAUGE

27 sts and 34 rows = 4" in St st, blocked.
20 sts and 34 rows = 4" over Muse Lace Pattern, blocked.

Muse Top

Notes:

Little details like buttons at the hem, and shoulder seams shifted to the front, make this top unique. Begin with a lace hem worked sideways. The front and back are picked up from this band, worked separately, and seamed. The same simple lace pattern is inserted at the centers front and back; the front panel fans out as you approach the neckline. Finally, sleeves are picked up and worked with short rows. You will wash and block three times throughout the pattern but don't be daunted, the results are well worth the extra effort.

Work the Charts from the bottom up, reading RS rows (odd numbers) from right to left and WS rows (even numbers) from left to right.

Lace Pattern (worked flat over an even number of sts)
Row 1 (RS): *K2tog, YO, rep from * to end.
Row 2 (WS): P.
Row 3: K1, *K2tog, YO, rep from * to last st, K1.
Row 4: P.
Rep Rows 1-4 for pattern.

Wrap and Turn (W&T): Tutorial on Knit Picks website can be found at http://tutorials.knitpicks.com/wptutorials/short-rows-wrap-and-turn-or-wt/

DIRECTIONS

Hem

CO 20 sts and work 7 rows of Garter St (K every row).
Setup Row (WS): K1, K2tog, *K2, K2tog; rep from * 4 times, K1. 15 sts.
Establish Lace Pattern as follows:
Row 1 (RS): K2, work Row 1 of Lace Pattern to the last st, K1.
Row 2: K1, P12 (Row 2 of Lace Pattern), K2.
Continue in this manner with center lace panel bordered with Garter St, 2 sts on the right hand side and 1 st on the left, for a total of 71 (80, 88, 97, 105, 114) Lace Pattern reps. Use row counter as a pattern rep counter.
Next Row (RS): K1, KFB, *K2, KFB; rep from * 4 times, K1. 20 sts.
Work 3 rows Garter St. Work button hole row as follows.
Button Hole Row (RS): K4, *K2tog, YO, K3; rep from * 3 times, K1.
Work 3 rows Garter St. BO.
Weave in ends, wash and block to 3" wide by 34.5 (38.5, 42.5, 46.5, 50.5, 54.5)", stretching only the Lace Panel length-wise so the Garter St sections along the short sides are each 0.5".

Front

Wrap Hem section into a circle with ends overlapping 0.5", being certain buttonholes are on top. Pin in place. Position so the RS and overlap are facing you and wider of the lengthwise Garter borders is at the bottom. Place markers along the single st Garter border: at 4.25 (4.75, 5.25, 5.75, 6.25, 6.75)" to the right of the BO button hole edge, 7 (8, 9, 10, 11, 12)" to the left of first marker, 3" to the left of second marker, 7 (8, 9, 10, 11, 12)" to the left of third marker. You have marked off three sections for the Front.

CO one st, then PU and K 47 (54, 61, 68, 74, 81) sts evenly across first section, when you come to the overlapped bands pickup

between both layers together. PU and K 16 sts evenly across second section and 47 (54, 61, 68, 74, 81) sts evenly across last section, CO 1 st. 110 (124, 138, 152, 164, 178) sts plus 1 selvedge st at each edge on needles.

Remove the outer markers.

Row 1 (WS): P.
Establish Lace Panel as follows.
Row 2 (RS): K to M, work Row 1 of Lace Pattern to M, K to the end.
Row 3: K1 selvedge st, P to last st (Row 2 of Lace Pattern), K1 selvedge st.

Continue in established pattern and work shaping as follows. Continuing row count as above, work 13 (13, 9, 9, 13, 13) rows, then work Decrease Row:
Decrease Row (RS): K2, SSK, work as established to last 4 sts, K2tog, K2. 2 sts dec.
Rep the last 14 (14, 10, 10, 14, 14) rows 2 (2, 3, 3, 2, 2) times more. 104 (118, 130, 144, 158, 172) sts plus 1 selvedge st at each edge. Work 1 (1, 3, 3, 1, 1) rows even.

Work 13 (13, 9, 9, 13, 13) rows, then work Increase Row:
Increase Row (RS): K3, M1, work as established to last 3 sts, M1, K3. 2 sts inc.
Rep the last 14 (14, 10, 10, 14, 14) rows 2 (2, 3, 3, 2, 2) times more. 110 (124, 138, 152, 164, 178) sts plus 1 selvedge st at each edge. Work 1 (1, 3, 3, 1, 1) rows even.

Armhole Shaping and Lace Fan

Read ahead through this section as shaping and lace fan are worked simultaneously for some sizes.

At the beginning of the next 2 rows, BO 3 (3, 4, 7, 8, 10) sts. 106 (120, 132, 140, 150, 160) total sts.
At the beginning of the next 2 rows, BO 2 (3, 4, 6, 8, 10) sts. 102 (114, 124, 128, 134, 140) total sts.

Decrease Row (RS): K2, SSK, work as established to last 4 sts, K2tog, K2. 2 sts dec.
Beginning with next RS row, work Decrease Row every RS row a total of 2 (2, 4, 6, 8, 10) times. 96 (108, 114, 114, 116, 118) sts. Continue straight.

AT THE SAME TIME: After Row 21 (21, 23, 28, 32, 34) of armhole, on next RS row begin Lace Fan as follows.

Lace Fan

Row 1 (RS): Work as established to 2 sts before M, move M to this position, *K2tog, YO, rep from * to M, remove M, K2tog, YO, K1, PM, work as established to the end.
Row 2 (WS): P.
Row 3: Work as established to 1 st before M, move M to this position, *K2tog, YO, rep from * to M, remove M, K2tog, YO, K1, PM, work as established to the end.
Row 4: P.
Rep Rows 3-4 a total of 11 (13, 14, 14, 14, 15) times. Almost the entire width of yoke is worked into Lace Fan.

BO all sts.

Back

To pick up along the other half of the hem band: with RS facing you, first place markers 7 (8, 9, 10, 11, 12)" in from either end (edges of Front pickup row). Follow directions as for Front from pick up row to armhole shaping.

Armhole Shaping

At the beginning of the next 2 rows, BO 3 (3, 4, 7, 8, 10) sts. 106 (120, 132, 140, 150, 160) sts.

At the beg of the next 2 rows, BO 2 (3, 4, 6, 8, 10) sts. 102 (114, 124, 128, 134, 140) sts.

Decrease Row (RS): K2, SSK, work as established to last 4 sts, K2tog, K2. 2 sts dec.

Beginning with next RS row, work Decrease Row every RS row a total of 2 (2, 4, 6, 8, 10) times. 96 (108, 114, 114, 116, 118) sts. Continue straight for 52 (56, 56, 56, 56, 56) rows. (You should have ended with a WS row.)

Shoulder Straps

K 21 (25, 27, 27, 29, 29) shoulder sts, BO 54(58, 60, 60, 58, 60) back of neck sts, K rem 21 (25, 27, 27, 29, 29) shoulder sts. Continue each shoulder strap for 12 more rows, BO all sts.

Weave in ends, wash and block to diagram, note that selvedge sts are not included in measurements. Sew side seams. Sew Shoulder Strap BO edges to Front BO edge, aligning armhole edges.

Neckline

Beginning at the corner between the back neck and left shoulder, PU and K all the way around the neck opening. Along the verticals of the shoulder straps PU at a rate of 4 sts for every 5 rows. Along the BO edges of Front and Back, PU 1 st for each BO st.

*P 1 rnd, K 1 rnd; rep from * three times.
BO K-wise.

Sleeves

Lay garment on a flat surface so Shoulder Straps are folded to the Front. Place M at top of armhole (where a normal shoulder seam would be). Join yarn at underarm seam. Using DPNs, PU and K 35 (37, 41, 46, 52, 57) sts evenly along armhole edge between underarm seam and M. Then PU and K the same number down the other half of the armhole edge. 70 (74, 82, 92, 104, 114) sts.

As you work Short Rows, whenever you come to a wrapped st, work the wrap tog with the st it is wrapping.

Short Row 1: K to 12 (12, 14, 15, 17, 19) sts past M, W&T.
Short Row 2: P 24 (24, 28, 30, 34, 38) sts, W&T.
Short Row 3: K 30 (30, 34, 36, 40, 44) sts, W&T.
Short Row 4: P 36 (36, 40, 42, 46, 50) sts, W&T.
Short Row 5: K 42 (42, 46, 47, 51, 55) sts, W&T.
Short Row 6: P 48 (48, 52, 52, 56, 60) sts, W&T.
Short Row 7: K 53 (53, 57, 57, 61, 64) sts, W&T.
Short Row 8: P 58 (58, 62, 62, 66, 68) sts, W&T.
Short Row 9: K 59 (59, 63, 63, 67, 69) sts, W&T.
Short Row 10: P 60 (60, 64, 64, 68, 70) sts, W&T.
Short Row 11: K 62 (61, 65, 65, 69, 71) sts, W&T.
Short Row 12: P 64 (62, 66, 66, 70, 72) sts, W&T.
Short Row 13: K 67 (65, 70, 72, 71, 73) sts, W&T.

Short Row 14: K (P, P, P, P, P) 70 (68, 74, 78, 72, 74) sts. Size 34.5 skip ahead to Cuff. Remaining sizes W&T.
Short Row 15: K -(71, 78, 85, 80, 84) sts, W&T.
Short Row 16: -(K, K, K, P, P) -(74, 82, 92, 88, 94) sts. Sizes 38.5, 42.5, and 46.5 skip ahead to Cuff. Remaining sizes W&T.
Short Row 17: K -(-, -, -, 96, 104) sts, W&T.
Short Row 18: K -(-, -, -, 104, 114) sts.

Cuff

*K 1 rnd, P 1 rnd.; rep from * twice.
BO K-wise.

Work second Sleeve in identical manner.

Finishing

Weave in ends, wash and block so sleeves are 1.5 (1.75, 1.75, 1.75, 2, 2)" at longest point. Sew buttons to Hem Band so they align with button holes.

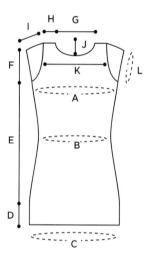

A 34.5 (38.5, 42.5, 46.5, 50.5, 54.5)"
B 32.5 (36.5, 40, 44.5, 48.5, 52.5)"
C 34 (38, 42, 46, 50, 54)"
D 3"
E 13"
F 7 (7.5, 8, 8.5, 9, 9.5)"
G 9 (9, 9.5, 9.5, 9.5, 9.5)"
H 3 (3.75, 4, 4, 4.25, 4.25)"
I 1.5 (1.75, 1.75, 1.75, 2, 2)"
J 1.5"
K 15 (16.5, 17.5, 17.5, 18, 18)"
L 10.25, (11, 12, 13.5, 15.5, 17)"

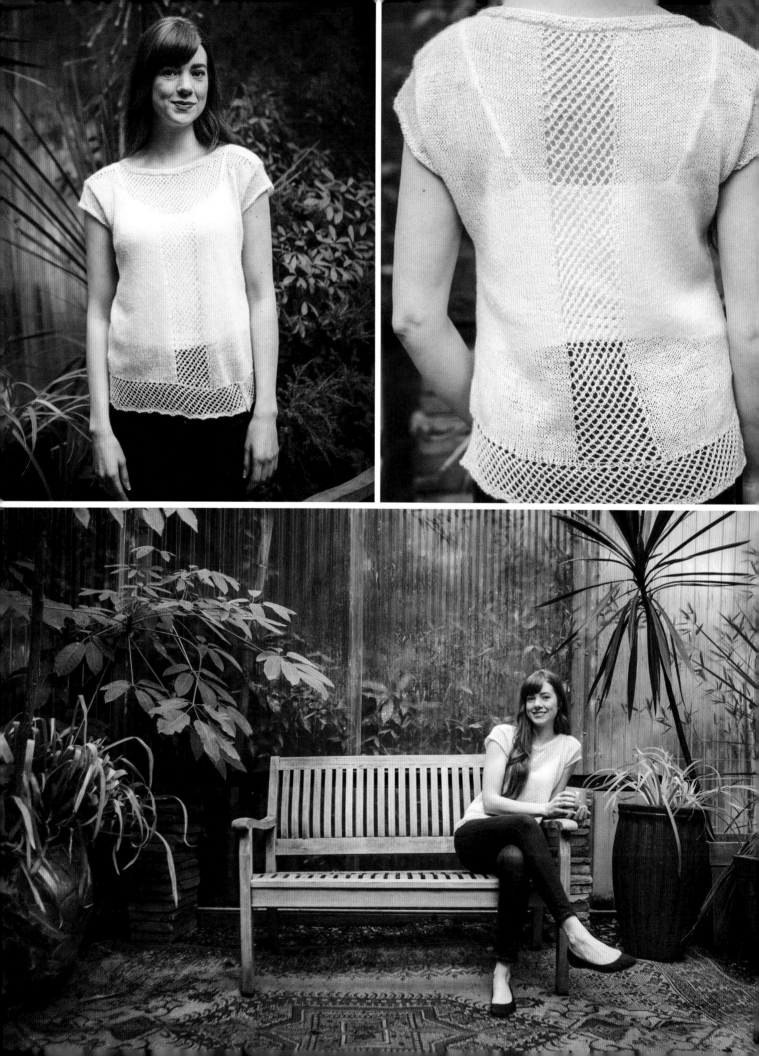

Muse Lace Fan Chart

	16	15	14	13	12	11	10	9	8	7	6	5	4	3	2	1	
4	◆	▨													▨	◆	
	◆		○	/	○	/	○	/	○	/	○	/	○	/		◆	3
2	◆	▨	▨											▨	▨	◆	
	◆			○	/	○	/	○	/	○	/	○	/			◆	1
	◆	▨	▨	▨								▨	▨	▨	▨	◆	
	◆	▨	▨	▨		○	/	○	/			▨	▨	▨	▨	◆	
	◆	▨	▨	▨								▨	▨	▨	▨	◆	
	◆	▨	▨	▨		○	/	○	/	○	/	▨	▨	▨	▨	◆	

Repeat Rows 1-4. The rows displayed below Row 1 represent the panel before the fan and are included here for reference only.

Muse Lace Chart

	8	7	6	5	4	3	2	1	
8									
		○	/	○	/	○	/		7
6									
	○	/	○	/	○	/	○	/	5
4									
		○	/	○	/	○	/		3
2									
	○	/	○	/	○	/	○	/	1

Legend

k2tog
RS: Knit two stitches together as one stitch
WS: Purl 2 stitches together

yo
yarn over

knit
RS: knit stitch
WS: purl stitch

pattern repeat

marker
moves out from center every RS row

No Stitch
Placeholder - No stitch made.

CHANTEUSE DRESS

by Nadya Stallings

FINISHED MEASUREMENTS

32 (36, 40, 44, 48, 52, 56, 60)" finished bust measurement; garment is meant to be worn with no ease.

YARN

Knit Picks Hawthorne Kettle Dye (80% Superwash Fine Highland Wool, 20% Polyamide (Nylon)/100g): Wisp 26692, 4 (4, 5, 5, 6, 6, 7, 7) skeins

NEEDLES

US 4 (3.5mm) 16" plus 24" or longer circular needles, or size to obtain gauge.

NOTIONS

Yarn Needle
Stitch Markers
Scrap Yarn or Stitch Holder
2 Row Counters

GAUGE

20 sts and 24 rows = 4" over Texture Stitch pattern, blocked.

Chanteuse Dress

Notes:

Each piece of this garment begins with a lace pattern, which further turns into a textural pattern by switching from YO to M1 stitch. Stitch patterns are both written and charted. Although the stitch pattern itself is not complicated, there is a chance of confusion and miscounting while working through decreases and increases. For this reason, it is necessary to pay close attention to which stitch pattern row is being worked. All stitches, except 6-stitch pattern repeats, need to be worked in St st, avoiding extra decreases or increases.

Read RS chart rows (odd numbers) from right to left.

Lace Stitch Pattern (worked flat over multiple of 6 sts, plus 2 sts for symmetry, plus 2 selvage sts)

Rows 1, 3, 5 (RS): Sl 1, *SSK, K2, YO, K2* to last 3 sts, K2, P1.
Row 2 and all even rows (WS): Sl 1, P to end of the row.
Rows 7, 9, 11: Sl 1, K1, *K2, YO, K2, K2tog* to last 2 sts, K1, P1.
Repeat Rows 1-12 for pattern.

Texture Stitch Pattern (worked flat over multiple of 6 sts, plus 2 sts for symmetry, plus 2 selvage sts)

Rows 1, 3, 5 (RS): Sl 1, *SSK, K2, M1, K2* to last 3 sts, K2, P1.
Row 2 and all even rows (WS): Sl 1, P to end of the row.
Rows 7, 9, 11: Sl 1, K1, *K2, M1, K2, K2tog* to last 2 sts, K1, P1.
Repeat Rows 1-12 for pattern.

Sewn Bind-off

Cut the working yarn to about 3 times as long as your finished piece of knitting. Thread that yarn onto blunt needle. *Pass the yarn needle through the first two sts from right to left. Pass the yarn needle through the first st on the knitting needle from left to right. Drop the first st off the knitting needle.* Repeat until one st remains. Sew through this last st from right to left.

Make One (M1): Increase one stitch using Loop Cast On technique: http://tutorials.knitpicks.com/wptutorials/category/getting-started/casting-on/

Wrap and Turn (W&T): Tutorial on Knit Picks website can be found at http://tutorials.knitpicks.com/wptutorials/short-rows-wrap-and-turn-or-wt/

DIRECTIONS

Back
The back is worked flat from the hem up.

Hem
CO 100 (112, 118, 130, 142, 154, 160, 172 sts.
Setup Row (WS): Sl 1, K to the last st, P1.
Beginning next row work Chart A Lace for 36 rows.
Beginning next row work Chart B Texture for 12 (10, 14, 12, 10, 8, 12, 10) rows ending with WS row.

Hem to Full Hip Decrease
Dec Row (RS): Sl 1, SSK, cont in pattern to last 3 sts, K2tog, P1. 2 sts dec.
Sl 1, SSK, cont in pattern to last 3 sts, K2tog, P1. 2 sts dec. Rep Dec Row every 12 (10, 14, 12, 10, 8, 0, 10)th row 4 (2, 2, 1, 2, 5, 0, 1) more times and then every 0 (8, 12, 10, 8, 6, 10, 8)th row 0 (3, 1, 3,

3, 1, 4, 4) more times. 90 (100, 110, 120, 130, 140, 150, 160) sts.
Cont in pattern for 21 (23, 23, 23, 23, 23, 23, 23) more rows ending with WS row.

Full Hip to Armhole Decrease
Dec Row (RS): Sl 1, SSK, cont in pattern to last 3 sts, K2tog, P1. 2 sts dec.
Sizes 32 (56, 60) ONLY: Rep Dec Row every 20 (22, 22)nd row 2 (1, 1) more times and then every 18 (20, 20)th row 2 (3, 3) more times.
Sizes 36 (40, 44, 48, 52) ONLY: Rep Dec Row every 20th row 4 more times.
80 (90, 100, 110, 120, 130, 140, 150) sts after working decreases.
Next Row (WS): Work in pattern.

Armhole Shaping
Working in pattern as established, BO 4 (4, 5, 5, 5, 6, 6, 7) sts in beginning of next two rows. 72 (82, 90, 100, 110, 118, 128, 136) sts.
Working in pattern as established, BO 3 sts in beginning of next two rows. Repeat 0 (0, 0, 0, 0, 1, 1, 1) more times. 66 (76, 84, 94, 104, 106, 116, 124) sts.
Working in pattern as established, BO 2 sts in beginning of the next 2 rows 0 (1, 1, 1, 1, 1, 2, 2) times. 66 (72, 80, 90, 100, 102, 108, 116) sts.
Dec Row (RS): Sl 1, SSK, work in pattern as established to last 3 sts, K2tog, P1. 2 sts dec.
Rep Dec Row every RS row 0 (1, 4, 7, 8, 9, 10, 14) more times ending with WS row. 64 (68, 70, 74, 82, 82, 86, 86) sts.
Cont in pattern for 38 (36, 32, 32, 30, 28, 26, 20) more rows ending with WS row.
BO 9 (10, 10, 10, 14, 14, 16, 16) sts in beginning of the next two rows. 46 (48, 50, 54, 54, 54, 54, 54) sts. Place remaining sts on stitch holder.

Front
Work as for Back until Armhole Shaping.

Armhole Shaping
Work as for Back for 24 (28, 30, 36, 36, 38, 40, 42) rows, ending with a WS row. 64 (68, 70, 74, 82, 82, 86, 86) sts.

Neckline Shaping
Beginning with next row, work armhole edge with no shaping until neckline shaping is completed. At the same time, begin Neckline Shaping, using short rows as follows:
Short Row 1 (RS): Work in pattern 27 (28, 28, 30, 34, 34, 36, 36) sts, w&t.
Short Rows 2. 4, 6, 8, 10, 12, 14, 16, 18, 20 (WS): Work in pattern to end.
Short Row 3: Work in pattern 23 (24, 24, 25, 29, 29, 31, 31) sts, w&t.
Short Row 5: Work in pattern 20 (20, 20, 21, 25, 25, 27, 27) sts, w&t.
Short Row 7: Work in pattern 17 (17, 17, 18, 22, 22, 24, 24) sts, w&t.
Short Row 9: Work in pattern 15 (15, 16, 16, 20, 20, 22, 22) sts, w&t.
Short Row 11: Work in pattern 14 (14, 14, 14, 18, 18, 20, 20) sts, w&t.
Short Row 13: Work in pattern 13 (13, 13, 13, 17, 17, 19, 19) sts, w&t.
Short Row 15: Work in pattern 12 (12, 12, 12, 16, 16, 18, 18) sts, w&t.
Short Row 17: Work in pattern 11 (11, 11, 11, 15, 15, 17, 17) sts, w&t.
Short Row 19: Work in pattern 10 (10, 10, 10, 14, 14, 16, 16) sts, w&t.

Short Row 21 (RS): Knit 28 (29 29, 31, 35, 35, 37, 37) sts, working wraps together with wrapped sts, cont in pattern to end of the row.

Short Row 22 (WS): Work in pattern 21 (22, 21, 23, 27, 27, 29, 29) sts, w&t.

Short Rows 23, 25, 27, 29, 31, 33, 35, 37, 39, 41 (RS): Work in pattern to end.

Short Row 24: Work in pattern 23 (24, 24, 25, 29, 29, 31, 31) sts, w&t.

Short Row 26: Work in pattern 20 (20, 20, 21, 25, 25, 27, 27) sts, w&t.

Short Row 28: Work in pattern 17 (17, 17, 18, 22, 22, 24, 24) sts, w&t.

Short Row 30: Work in pattern 15 (15, 16, 16, 20, 20, 22, 22) sts, w&t.

Short Row 32: Work in pattern 14 (14, 14, 14, 18, 18, 20, 20) sts, w&t.

Short Row 34: Work in pattern 13 (13, 13, 13, 17, 17, 19, 19) sts, w&t.

Short Row 36: Work in pattern 12 (12, 12, 12, 16, 16, 18, 18) sts, w&t.

Short Row 38: Work in pattern 11 (11, 11, 11, 15, 15, 17, 17) sts, w&t.

Short Row 40: Work in pattern 10 (10, 10, 10, 14, 14, 16, 16) sts, w&t.

Next Row (WS): BO 9 (10, 10, 10, 14, 14, 16, 16) shoulder sts, P to end of the row, working wraps together with wrapped sts to last 9 (10, 10, 10, 14, 14, 16, 16) sts. BO remaining 9 (10, 10, 10, 14, 14, 16, 16) shoulder sts.

Place 46 (48, 50, 54, 54, 54, 54, 54) remaining neck sts on scrap yarn or stitch holder.

Sleeves (make two)

The sleeves are worked flat from the cuffs up.

Cuff

CO 34 (34, 40, 40, 46, 46, 52, 52) sts.

Setup Row (WS): Sl 1, K to the last st, P1.

Beginning next row work Chart A Lace for 24 rows.

Beginning next row work Chart B Texture for 6 (4, 4, 4, 4, 4, 4, 4) rows ending with WS row.

Inc Row (RS): Sl 1, M1, work in pattern to last st, M1, P1. 2 sts inc.

Rep Inc row every 6 (4, 4, 4, 4, 4, 4, 4)th row 2 (13, 12, 7, 8, 5, 6, 4) more times and then every 4 (2, 2, 2, 2, 2, 2, 2)nd row 9 (1, 4, 14, 12, 18, 16, 21) more times. 58 (64, 74, 84, 88, 94, 98, 104) sts.

Next Row (WS): Work in pattern.

BO 4 (4, 5, 5, 5, 6, 6, 7) sts in beginning of next two rows. 50 (56, 64, 74, 78, 82, 86, 90) sts.

BO 3 sts in beginning of next two rows 1 (1, 1, 1, 1, 2, 2, 2) times. 44 (50, 58, 68, 72, 70, 74, 78) sts.

BO 2 sts in beginning of the next 2 rows 0 (1, 1, 1, 1, 1, 2, 2) times. 44 (46, 54, 64, 68, 66, 66, 70) sts.

Shape Sleeve Cap

Dec Row (RS): Sl 1, SSK, work in pattern to last 3 sts, K2tog, P1. 2 sts dec.

Rep Dec Row every other row 5 (5, 4, 4, 1, 3, 3, 2) more times. 32 (34, 44, 54, 64, 58, 58, 64) sts.

Next Row (WS): Work in pattern.

BO 2 sts in beginning of the next 2 rows 2 (2, 4, 5, 7, 5, 5, 6) times. 24 (26, 28, 34, 36, 38, 38, 40) sts.

BO 2 sts in beginning of the next 2 rows, and then BO 2 (2, 2, 3, 3, 3, 3, 3) sts in beginning of next 4 rows. 12 (14, 16, 18, 20, 22, 22, 24) sts. BO all remaining sts.

Finishing

Weave in ends, block pieces to schematic measurements. Sew shoulder seams. Sew sleeves into open armholes. Sew side seam and sleeve seam on each side.

Neckline Band

Beginning at the back center, place all live sts of the neckline on the shorter circular needle. PM and join to work in the round.

Round 1: Knit.

Round 2: Purl.

BO with sewn BO technique.

Block garment one more time if desired.

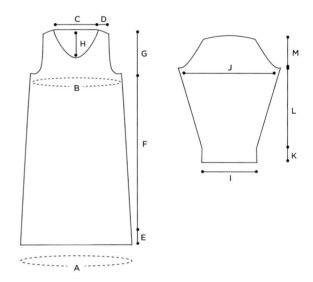

A 40 (45, 47, 52, 57, 61.5, 64, 69)"
B 32 (36, 40, 44, 48, 52, 56, 60)"
C 9.25 (9.5, 10, 10.75, 10.75, 10.75, 10.75, 10.75)"
D 1.75 (2, 2, 2, 2.75, 2.75, 3.25, 3.25)"
E 6"
F 26"
G 7 (7.5, 8, 9, 9, 9.25, 9.5, 10)"
H 3"
I 6.75 (6.75, 8, 8, 9.25, 9.25, 10.5, 10.5)"
J 11.5 (12.75, 14.75, 16.75, 17.5, 18.75, 19.5, 20.75)"
K 4"
L 9 (9.5, 10, 10, 10, 10, 10, 10.25)"
M 5 (5.25, 5.5, 6, 6, 6.25, 6.25, 6.25)"

Chart A Lace

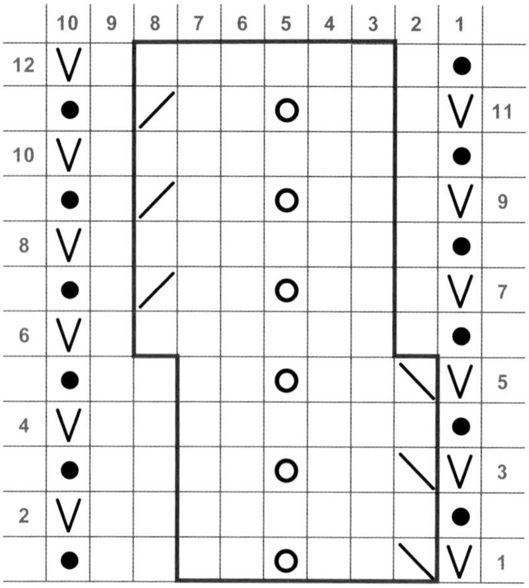

	10	9	8	7	6	5	4	3	2	1	
12	V									●	
		●	/			O				V	11
10	V									●	
		●	/			O				V	9
8	V									●	
		●	/			O				V	7
6	V									●	
		●				O			\	V	5
4	V									●	
		●				O			\	V	3
2	V									●	
		●				O			\	V	1

Chart B Texture

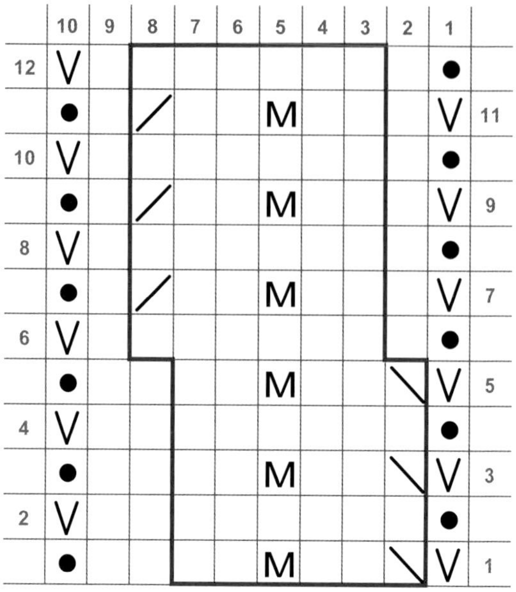

	10	9	8	7	6	5	4	3	2	1	
12	V									●	
		●	/			M				V	11
10	V									●	
		●	/			M				V	9
8	V									●	
		●	/			M				V	7
6	V									●	
		●				M			\	V	5
4	V									●	
		●				M			\	V	3
2	V									●	
		●				M			\	V	1

Legend

slip
V
RS: Slip stitch as if to purl, holding yarn in back
WS: Slip stitch as if to purl, holding yarn in front

ssk
\
RS: Slip one stitch as if to knit, Slip another stitch as if to knit. Insert left-hand needle into front of these 2 stitches and knit them together
WS: Purl two stitches together in back loops, inserting needle from the left, behind and into the backs of the 2nd & 1st stitches in that order

knit
RS: knit stitch
WS: purl stitch

yo
O
yarn over

purl
●
purl stitch

k2tog
/
RS: Knit two stitches together as one stitch
WS: Purl 2 stitches together

make one
M
Increase one stitch using the Loop Cast On

pattern repeat

FAIRY TALE TOP

by Katy Banks

FINISHED MEASUREMENTS

32 (34, 36, 38, 40, 42, 44, 46, 48, 50, 52, 54)" finished bust measurement; garment is meant to be worn with 2" of positive ease.

YARN

Knit Picks Shine Sport (60% Pima Cotton, 40% Modal®; 110 yards/50g): Clarity 26677, 8 (8, 8, 9, 9, 9, 10, 10, 11, 11, 11, 11) balls.

NEEDLES

US 6 (4mm) straight or circular needles plus spare DPN or straight needle, or size to obtain gauge.
US 5 (3.75mm) DPNs or two 24" circular needles for two circulars technique, or one size smaller than needle to obtain gauge.

NOTIONS

Yarn Needle
Stitch Marker (optional)
Scrap Yarn or Stitch Holder

GAUGE

21 sts and 28 rows = 4" in St st on larger needles, blocked.

Fairy Tale Top

Notes:

This stylish open-backed top is worked in pieces from the bottom up and seamed together. The top is knit in stockinette with a neat ribbed trim. The back panels are shaped using short rows, increases and decreases, and short rows are also used to shape the shoulders to create a neat 3-Needle BO seam.

1x1 Rib (worked flat or in the rnd over an even number of sts)
Every Row/Round: *K1, P1, rep from * to end.

1x1 Rib (worked flat over an odd number of sts)
Row 1: K1, *P1, K1, rep from * to end.
Row 2: P1, *K1, P1, rep from * to end.
Rep Rows 1-2 for pattern.

DIRECTIONS
Front

Using larger needles, CO 1 selvedge st, CO 94 (100, 106, 110, 116, 120, 126, 132, 136, 142, 148, 152) sts, CO 1 selvedge st. From this point on, the selvedge sts will not be mentioned or included in any st counts; they should be K on every row to create a neat edge for sewing later.
Work 10 rows 1x1 Rib.

Change to St st (K on RS, P on WS) and work 14 rows even, then work Decrease Rows as follows.
Decrease Row (RS): K1, SSK, K to last 3 sts, K2tog, K1. 2 sts dec. P one WS row.
Repeat the last 16 rows 5 times more, then work 16 (12, 14, 12, 12, 10, 12, 8, 10, 6, 6, 2) rows even. 82 (88, 94, 98, 104, 108, 114, 120, 124, 130, 136, 140) sts.

Armhole Shaping

At the beginning of the next 2 rows, BO 2 (3, 3, 3, 4, 4, 4, 5, 6, 6, 8, 8) sts. At the beginning of the next 2 rows BO - (-, -, 2, 2, 3, 4, 5, 6, 6, 7, 8) sts (if no number shown, skip these rows). 78 (82, 88, 88, 92, 94, 98, 100, 100, 106, 106, 108) sts.
Decrease Row (RS): K1, SSK, K to last 3 sts, K2tog, K1. 2 sts dec. Work a Decrease Row every RS row a total of 2 (2, 2, 2, 2, 4, 4, 4, 6, 6, 8) times. 74 (78, 84, 84, 88, 90, 90, 92, 92, 94, 94, 92) sts. Work 34 (38, 38, 38, 38, 42, 38, 42, 42, 40, 42, 42) rows even, then work a WS row.

Neckline Shaping

Row 1 (RS): K 26 (29, 30, 30, 32, 34, 35, 36, 36, 37, 37, 37) left shoulder sts, BO 22 (20, 24, 24, 24, 22, 20, 20, 20, 20, 20, 18) center sts, K rem 26 (29, 30, 30, 32, 34, 35, 36, 36, 37, 37, 37) right shoulder sts to end.
Row 2 (WS): P across right shoulder sts; join a second ball of yarn to left shoulder, BO 10 (10, 11, 11, 11, 10, 10, 10, 10, 10, 10, 10), P to end. 16 (19, 19, 19, 21, 24, 25, 26, 26, 27, 27, 27) left shoulder sts. Instructions are given for Left and Right Shoulders, worked with separate balls of yarn across the row.
Row 3: K to the last 3 sts of left shoulder, K2tog, K1; BO 10 (10, 11, 11, 11, 10, 10, 10, 10, 10, 10, 10) sts of right shoulder, K1, SSK, K to end. 15 (18, 18, 18, 20, 23, 24, 25, 25, 26, 26, 26) sts on each shoulder.
Row 4: P to the last 3 sts of right shoulder, SSP, P1; for left shoulder, P1, P2tog, P to end. 1 st dec each shoulder.

Shoulder Shaping

Whenever you come to a wrapped st, work wrap tog with st it is wrapping.
For left shoulder:
Short Row 1 (RS): K 5 (6, 6, 6, 7, 8, 8, 8, 9, 9, 9), W&T.
Short Row 2 (WS): P.
Short Row 3: K 10 (12, 12, 12, 14, 16, 16, 16, 18, 18, 18, 18), W&T.
Short Row 4: P.
Row 5: K.
Row 6: P.
For right shoulder:
Row 1: K.
Short Row 2: P 5 (6, 6, 6, 7, 8, 8, 8, 9, 9, 9), W&T.
Short Row 3: K.
Short Row 4: P 10 (12, 12, 12, 14, 16, 16, 16, 18, 18, 18, 18), W&T.
Row 5: K.
Row 6: P.
Place shoulder sts on scrap yarn or stitch holders. 14 (17, 17, 17, 19, 22, 23, 24, 24, 25, 25, 25) sts.

Right Back

Hem

Using long-tail method, CO 1 selvedge st, CO 47 (49, 53, 55, 57, 59, 63, 65, 67, 71, 73, 75) more sts. This counts as Row 1. From this point on, the selvedge st will not be mentioned or included in any st counts; it should be K on every row to create a neat edge for sewing later.
Throughout the following short rows, you will work each st column in the rib pattern for 10 rows, then switch to St st, with the exception of the 6 sts along the center back edge which will stay in rib pattern. Whenever you come to a wrapped st, work the wrap tog with the st it is wrapping.
Finally, you will begin working increases along the center edge. Also, you may find it useful after a few rows to place a marker on the RS.
Short Row 2 (WS): P1, K1, W&T.
Short Row 3 and all odd (RS) Rows not specified below: Work in 1x1 Rib or St st, as established in the row below.
Short Row 4: Work 6 (6, 6, 7, 7, 7, 7, 7, 8, 8, 8) sts in 1x1 Rib, W&T.
Short Row 6: Work 10 (10, 10, 11, 12, 12, 12, 12, 14, 14, 14) sts in 1x1 Rib, W&T.
Short Row 7: Work as established to the last 6 sts, M1 (0, 1, 1, 1, 0, 0, 0, 0, 0, 0), work last 6 sts as established.
Short Row 8: Work 6 sts in 1x1 Rib, M0 (1, 0, 0, 0, 0, 1, 1, 1, 1, 0), K1 (0, 1, 1, 1, 0, 0, 0, 0, 0, 0), work 8 (8, 8, 9, 11, 11, 11, 11, 14, 14, 14) sts as established in 1x1 Rib, W&T.
Short Row 9: Work as established to the last 6 sts, M0 (0, 0, 0, 0, 0, 0, 0, 0, 0, 1), work last 6 sts as established.
Short Row 10: Work 6 sts in 1x1 Rib, K1, work 12 (12, 12, 13, 15, 16, 16, 16, 16, 20, 20, 20) sts in 1x1 Rib, W&T.
Short Row 12: Work 6 sts in 1x1 Rib, P1, work 16 (16, 16, 17, 18, 21, 21, 21, 21, 25, 26, 26) sts in 1x1 Rib, W&T.
Short Row 14: Work 6 sts in 1x1 Rib, M1 (0, 1, 1, 1, 1, 0, 0, 0, 0, 0, 0), P1 (1, 1, 1, 1, 1, 1, 1, 3, 3, 3), work 20 (20, 20, 21, 23, 25, 26, 26, 26, 28, 30, 30) sts in 1x1 Rib, W&T.
Short Row 16: Work 6 sts in 1x1 Rib, M0 (1, 0, 0, 0, 0, 1, 1, 1, 1, 0), P6 (5, 6, 7, 8, 8, 7, 7, 7, 9, 9, 9), work 19 (20, 20, 21, 23, 23, 25, 25, 25, 27, 29, 30) sts in 1x1 Rib, W&T.

Short Row 18: Work 6 sts in 1x1 Rib, M0 (0, 0, 0, 0, 0, 0, 0, 0, 0, 0, 1), P10 (10, 10, 11, 13, 13, 13, 13, 13, 16, 16, 15), work 18 (20, 20, 20, 20, 22, 25, 25, 25, 26, 28, 30) sts in 1x1 Rib, W&T.

Short Row 20: Work 6 sts in 1x1 Rib, P14 (14, 14, 15, 17, 18, 18, 18, 18, 22, 22, 22), work 17 (19, 20, 20, 21, 21, 25, 25, 25, 27, 29) sts in 1x1 Rib, W&T.

Short Row 21: Work as established to the last 6 sts, M1 (0, 1, 1, 1, 1, 0, 0, 0, 0, 0, 0), work last 6 sts as established. 49 (51, 55, 57, 59, 61, 65, 67, 69, 73, 75, 77) sts.

Short Row 22: Work 6 sts in 1x1 Rib, P19 (18, 19, 20, 22, 23, 23, 23, 23, 27, 28, 28), work 16 (18, 20, 20, 20, 20, 24, 25, 25, 25, 26, 28) sts in 1x1 Rib, W&T.

Short Row 24: Work 6 sts in 1x1 Rib, M0 (1, 0, 0, 0, 0, 1, 1, 1, 1, 1, 0), P23 (22, 23, 24, 26, 28, 28, 28, 28, 32, 34, 34), work 15 (17, 20, 20, 20, 20, 23, 25, 25, 25, 25, 27) sts in 1x1 Rib, W&T.

Short Row 26: Work 6 sts in 1x1 Rib, P26 (27, 27, 28, 30, 32, 34, 34, 34, 38, 40, 40), work 15 (16, 20, 20, 20, 20, 22, 24, 25, 25, 25, 26) sts in 1x1 Rib, W&T.

Short Row27: Work as established to the last 6 sts, M0 (0, 0, 0, 0, 0, 0, 0, 0, 0, 0, 1), work last 6 sts as established.

Short Row 28: Work 6 sts in 1x1 Rib, M1 (0, 1, 1, 1, 1, 0, 0, 0, 0, 0, 0), P29 (31, 31, 32, 34, 36, 39, 39, 39, 43, 45, 47), work remaining 15 (15, 19, 20, 20, 20, 21, 23, 25, 25, 25, 25) sts in 1x1 Rib. 50 (52, 56, 58, 60, 62, 66, 68, 70, 74, 76, 78) sts.

Body

Rows 1, 3 and 5 (RS): Work in St st or 1x1 Rib as established in row below.

Row 2 (WS): Work 6 sts in 1x1 Rib, P33 (34, 35, 36, 38, 40, 42, 42, 42, 46, 48, 50), work 1x1 Rib to end.

Row 4: Work 6 sts in 1x1 Rib, M0 (1, 0, 0, 0, 0, 0, 1, 1, 1, 1, 0), P36 (37, 39, 40, 42, 44, 46, 47, 47, 51, 53, 55), work 1x1 Rib to end.

Row 6: Work 6 sts in 1x1 Rib, P39 (41, 44, 45, 47, 49, 53, 55, 55, 59, 61, 62), work 1x1 Rib to end.

Row 7: Work 6 (6, 7, 8, 8, 8, 8, 10, 10, 10, 10) in 1x1 Rib, work as established to the last 6 sts, M1 (0, 1, 1, 1, 1, 0, 0, 0, 0, 0, 0), work as established to the end.

Row 8: Work 6 sts in 1x1 Rib, M0 (0, 0, 0, 0, 1, 0, 0, 0, 0, 1), P43 (44, 49, 50, 52, 53, 57, 59, 60, 64, 66, 67), work 1x1 Rib to end. 51 (53, 57, 59, 61, 63, 67, 69, 71, 75, 77, 78) sts.

Read ahead through this section as side seam decreases and armhole shaping are worked simultaneously with center back increases. From this point on, only the 6 center edge sts are worked in rib; the rest in St st.

Work center edge increases as follows.
Work 5 (3, 5, 5, 5, 5, 8, 3, 3, 3, 3, 3) rows with center edge even.
Work one Increase Row by inserting M1 between the rib and St st sections (this can be done on a RS or WS row). 1 st inc.
Work 7 (7, 6, 6, 6, 7, 7, 7, 7, 7, 8) rows even.
Work one Increase Row as described above. 1 st inc.
Repeat the last 8 (8, 7, 7, 8, 8, 8, 8, 8, 8, 9) rows 19 (8, 15, 15, 5, 19, 4, 4, 2, 2, 2, 16) times more.
Sizes 32 and 42, no more center increases.
All other sizes: Work - (8, 7, 7, -, 8, 8, 8, 8, 8, 9) rows even. Work one Increase Row as described above. Repeat the last - (9, 8, 8, 8, -, 9, 9, 9, 9, 9, -) rows - (9, 5, 5, 14, -, 13, 13, 15, 15, 15, -) times more. 21 (20, 23, 23, 22, 21, 19, 19, 20, 20, 20, 19) center edge sts inc.

AT THE SAME TIME:
Work side edge decreases as follows.
After Body Row 8 above, work 15 rows keeping the side edge even.
Work one Decrease Row (WS) by working to the last 3 sts, SSP, P1. 1 st dec.
Repeat the last 16 rows 5 times more (6 side edge sts dec), then work 16 (12, 14, 12, 12, 10, 12, 8, 10, 6, 6, 2) rows keeping the side edge even, or until length from short edge is 17.5 (17, 17.25, 16.75, 17, 16.5, 16.75, 16.25, 16.5, 16, 16, 15.5)", ending with a WS row.

Armhole Shaping

The side edge should be the same length as the front side edge. Continue center edge increases as described above. At the beginning of the next row (RS), BO 2 (3, 3, 4, 4, 4, 4, 5, 6, 6, 8, 8) sts. Work 1 WS row.
At the beginning of the next RS row BO - (-, -, 2, 2, 3, 4, 5, 6, 6, 7, 8) sts (if no number shown, skip these rows). Work 1 WS Row.
Work Decrease Row by working K1, SSK at the beginning of every RS row 2 (2, 2, 2, 2, 4, 4, 4, 6, 6, 8) times. 4 (5, 5, 7, 8, 9, 12, 14, 16, 18, 21, 24) sts BO and dec at armhole.
Work 34 (38, 38, 40, 40, 44, 40, 42, 42, 42, 44, 42) rows keeping armhole edge even, ending on a WS row.

62 (62, 69, 69, 69, 69, 68, 68, 69, 71, 70, 67) sts after completing all shaping.

Shoulder Shaping

Continue center edge increases as described above. Whenever you come to a wrapped st, work wrap tog with st it is wrapping.
For right shoulder:

Short Row 1: K 5 (6, 6, 6, 7, 8, 8, 8, 9, 9, 9), W&T.

Short Row 2: P.

Short Row 3: K 10 (12, 12, 12, 14, 16, 16, 16, 18, 18, 18, 18), W&T.

Short Row 4: P.

Short Row 5: K 16 (19, 18, 19, 21, 24, 25, 25, 27, 27, 27, 27), W&T.

Short Row 6: P.

You should have completed center edge increases. Place sts on spare needle or, if you have a second circular, set this piece aside and work the Left Back on this second needle.

Left Back

Hem

Using long-tail method, CO 47 (49, 53, 55, 57, 59, 63, 65, 67, 71, 73, 75) sts, CO 1 selvedge st. From this point on, the selvedge st will not be mentioned or included in any st counts; it should be K on every row to create a neat edge for sewing later.
Next row, work 1x1 Rib. This counts as Row 1. Just as for Right Back, you will work each st column in the rib pattern for 10 rows, then switch to St st, with the exception of the 6 sts along the center back edge which will stay in rib pattern. Whenever you come to a wrapped st, work the wrap tog with the st it is wrapping.
Finally, you will begin working increases along the center edge. Also, you may find it useful after a few rows to place a marker in the RS.

Short Row 2 (RS): K1, P1, W&T.

Short Row 3 and all odd (WS) Rows not specified below: Work in 1x1 Rib or St st, as established in the row below.

Short Row 4: Work 6 (6, 6, 7, 7, 7, 7, 7, 8, 8, 8) sts in 1x1 Rib, W&T.

Short Row 6: Work 10 (10, 10, 11, 12, 12, 12, 12, 12, 14, 14, 14) sts in 1x1 Rib, W&T.

Short Row 7: Work as established to the last 6 sts, M1 (0, 1, 1, 1, 1, 0, 0, 0, 0, 0, 0), work last 6 sts as established.

Short Row 8: Work 6 sts in 1x1 Rib, M0 (1, 0, 0, 0, 0, 1, 1, 1, 1, 1, 0), P1 (0, 1, 1, 1, 1, 0, 0, 0, 0, 0, 0), work 8 (8, 8, 9, 11, 11, 11, 11, 11, 14, 14, 14) sts as established in 1x1 Rib, W&T.

Short Row 9: Work as established to the last 6 sts, M0 (0, 0, 0, 0, 0, 0, 0, 0, 0, 0, 1), work last 6 sts as established.

Short Row 10: Work 6 sts in 1x1 Rib, P1, work 12 (12, 12, 13, 15, 16, 16, 16, 16, 20, 20, 20) sts in 1x1 Rib, W&T.

Short Row 12: Work 6 sts in 1x1 Rib, K1, work 16 (16, 16, 17, 18, 21, 21, 21, 21, 25, 26, 26) sts in 1x1 Rib, W&T.

Short Row 14: Work 6 sts in 1x1 Rib, M1 (0, 1, 1, 1, 1, 0, 0, 0, 0, 0, 0), K1 (1, 1, 1, 1, 1, 1, 1, 3, 3, 3), work 20 (20, 20, 21, 23, 25, 26, 26, 26, 28, 30, 30) sts in 1x1 Rib, W&T.

Short Row 16: Work 6 sts in 1x1 Rib, M0 (1, 0, 0, 0, 0, 1, 1, 1, 1, 1, 0), K6 (5, 6, 7, 8, 7, 7, 7, 9, 9, 9), work 19 (20, 20, 21, 23, 23, 25, 25, 25, 27, 29, 30) sts in 1x1 Rib, W&T.

Short Row 18: Work 6 sts in 1x1 Rib, M0 (0, 0, 0, 0, 0, 0, 0, 0, 0, 0, 1), K10 (10, 10, 11, 13, 13, 13, 13, 13, 16, 16, 15), work 18 (20, 20, 20, 22, 25, 25, 25, 26, 28, 30) sts in 1x1 Rib, W&T.

Short Row 20: Work 6 sts in 1x1 Rib, K14 (14, 14, 15, 17, 18, 18, 18, 18, 22, 22, 22), work 17 (19, 20, 20, 21, 21, 25, 25, 25, 27, 29) sts in 1x1 Rib, W&T.

Short Row 21: Work as established to the last 6 sts, M1 (0, 1, 1, 1, 1, 0, 0, 0, 0, 0, 0), work last 6 sts as established. 49 (51, 55, 57, 59, 61, 65, 67, 69, 73, 75, 77) sts.

Short Row 22: Work 6 sts in 1x1 Rib, K19 (18, 19, 20, 22, 23, 23, 23, 23, 27, 28, 28), work 16 (18, 20, 20, 20, 20, 24, 25, 25, 25, 26, 28) sts in 1x1 Rib, W&T.

Short Row 24: Work 6 sts in 1x1 Rib, M0 (1, 0, 0, 0, 0, 1, 1, 1, 1, 1, 0), K23 (22, 23, 24, 26, 28, 28, 28, 28, 32, 34, 34), work 15 (17, 20, 20, 20, 20, 23, 25, 25, 25, 25, 27) sts in 1x1 Rib, W&T.

Short Row 26: Work 6 sts in 1x1 Rib, K26 (27, 27, 28, 30, 32, 34, 34, 34, 38, 40, 40), work 15 (16, 20, 20, 20, 20, 22, 24, 25, 25, 25, 26) sts in 1x1 Rib, W&T.

Short Row 27: Work as established to the last 6 sts, M0 (0, 0, 0, 0, 0, 0, 0, 0, 0, 0, 1), work last 6 sts as established.

Short Row 28: Work 6 sts in 1x1 Rib, M1 (0, 1, 1, 1, 1, 0, 0, 0, 0, 0, 0), K29 (31, 31, 32, 34, 36, 39, 39, 39, 43, 45, 47), work remaining 15 (15, 19, 20, 20, 20, 21, 23, 25, 25, 25, 25) sts in 1x1 Rib. 50 (52, 56, 58, 60, 62, 66, 68, 70, 74, 76, 78) sts.

Body

Rows 1, 3 and 5 (WS): Work in St st or 1x1 Rib as established in row below.

Row 2 (RS): Work 6 sts in 1x1 Rib, K33 (34, 35, 36, 38, 40, 42, 42, 42, 46, 48, 50), work 1x1 Rib to end.

Row 4: Work 6 sts in 1x1 Rib, M0 (1, 0, 0, 0, 0, 0, 1, 1, 1, 1, 0), K36 (37, 39, 40, 42, 44, 46, 47, 47, 51, 53, 55), work 1x1 Rib to end.

Row 6: Work 6 sts in 1x1 Rib, K39 (41, 44, 45, 47, 49, 53, 55, 55, 59, 61, 62), work 1x1 Rib to end.

Row 7: Work 6 (6, 7, 8, 8, 8, 8, 10, 10, 10, 10) in 1x1 Rib, work as established to the last 6 sts, M1 (0, 1, 1, 1, 1, 0, 0, 0, 0, 0, 0), work as established to the end.

Row 8: Work 6 sts in 1x1 Rib, M0 (0, 0, 0, 0, 1, 0, 0, 0, 0, 0, 1), K43 (44, 49, 50, 52, 53, 57, 59, 60, 64, 66, 67), work 1x1 Rib to end. 51 (53, 57, 59, 61, 63, 67, 69, 71, 75, 77, 78) sts.

Read ahead through this section as side seam decreases and armhole shaping are worked simultaneously with center back increases. From this point on, only the 6 center edge sts are worked in rib; the rest in St st.

Work center edge increases as follows.
Work 5 (3, 5, 5, 5, 5, 8, 3, 3, 3, 3, 3) rows with center edge even. Work one Increase Row by inserting M1 between the rib and St st sections. 1 st inc.
Work 7 (7, 6, 6, 6, 7, 7, 7, 7, 7, 8) rows even.
Work one Increase Row as described above.
Repeat the last 8 (8, 7, 7, 7, 8, 8, 8, 8, 8, 8, 9) rows 19 (8, 15, 15, 5, 19, 4, 4, 2, 2, 2, 16) times more.
Sizes 32 and 42, no more center increases.
All other sizes: Work - (8, 7, 7, 7, -, 8, 8, 8, 8, 8, 9) rows even. Work one Increase Row as described above. Repeat the last - (9, 8, 8, 8, -, 9, 9, 9, 9, 9, -) rows - (9, 5, 5, 14, -, 13, 13, 15, 15, 15, -) times more. 21 (20, 23, 23, 22, 21, 19, 19, 20, 20, 20, 19) center edge sts inc.

AT THE SAME TIME:
Work side edge decreases as follows. After Body Row 8 above, work 15 rows keeping the side edge even. Work one Decrease Row by working to the last 3 sts, SSK, K1. Repeat the last 16 rows 5 times more, then work 16 (12, 14, 12, 12, 10, 12, 8, 10, 6, 6, 2) rows keeping the side edge even.

Armhole Shaping

The side edge should be the same length as the front side edge. Continue center edge increases as described above. At the beginning of the next row, BO 2 (3, 3, 3, 4, 4, 4, 5, 6, 6, 8, 8) sts. At the beginning of the next WS row BO - (-, -, 2, 2, 3, 4, 5, 6, 6, 7, 8) sts (if no number shown, skip these rows). Work Decrease Row by working SSP, P1 at the end of every WS row 2 (2, 2, 2, 2, 4, 4, 4, 6, 6, 8) times. Work 34 (38, 38, 40, 40, 44, 40, 42, 42, 42, 44, 42) rows keeping armhole edge even, ending on a RS row.

Shoulder Shaping

Continue center edge increases as described above. Whenever you come to a wrapped st, work wrap tog with st it is wrapping. For right shoulder:

Short Row 1: P 5 (6, 6, 6, 7, 8, 8, 8, 9, 8, 9), W&T.

Short Row 2: K.

Short Row 3: P 10 (12, 12, 12, 14, 16, 16, 16, 18, 18, 18, 18), W&T.

Short Row 4: K.

Short Row 5: P 16 (19, 18, 19, 21, 24, 25, 25, 27, 27, 27, 27), W&T.

Short Row 6: K.

You should have completed center edge increases.

62 (62, 69, 69, 69, 69, 68, 68, 69, 71, 70, 67) sts after completing all shaping.

Finishing

Joining Shoulders and Back of Neck

It will be much easier if the pieces are laid on a flat surface. Lay Front with RS up, move Front shoulder sts to DPNs. Lay Left Back piece on top of Front with WS up and aligning shoulder sts.

Lay Right Back piece upside down with RS up, above the other pieces so the live sts are parallel to those of the other pieces. Work 3-Needle BO to join 16 (19, 19, 19, 21, 24, 25, 26, 26, 27, 27, 27) shoulder sts, including selvedge sts. Slip the last st worked to the left hand needle. Lift the Left Back up, opening the seam just completed, and lay it on top of the Right Back. Both back pieces are now upside down with RS up. Return Sl st to RH needle and continue 3-Needle BO to join 46 (43, 50, 50, 48, 45, 43, 42, 43, 44, 43, 40) back of neck pieces. Sl the last st worked to the left hand needle. Return the Left Back to its original position (opening the back of neck join just created), then fold the Right Back along the joins just created and lay it on top of the other pieces, WS will now be facing up. Return the Sl st to RH needle and continue 3-Needle BO to join the remaining 16 (19, 19, 19, 21, 24, 25, 26, 26, 27, 27, 27) shoulder sts, including selvedge sts. Secure the last st.

Neck and Armhole Trim

Weave in ends, wash and block to diagram (note the selvedge sts are not included in the given measurements).

With smaller needles, RS facing you, and beginning at the left shoulder seam, PU and K around neck opening at a rate of 4 sts for every 5 rows and 1 st for every BO st. Adjust as necessary to obtain an even number of sts.

Work 1x1 Rib for 4 rnds, BO loosely.

Sew side seams.

In the same manner as for the neck and beginning at the side seam, PU and K around armhole opening.

Work 1x1 Rib for 4 rnds, BO loosely. Repeat for other armhole.

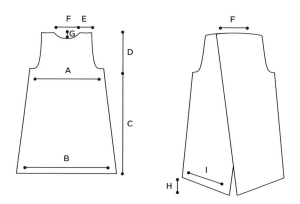

A 15.5 (16.75, 18, 18.75, 19.75, 20.5, 21.75, 22.75, 23.5, 24.75, 26, 26.75)″
B 18 (19, 20.25, 21, 22, 22.75, 24, 25.25, 26, 27, 28.25, 29)″
C 17.5 (16.75, 17.25, 16.75, 16.75, 16.5, 16.75, 16.25, 16.5, 16, 16, 15.5)″
D 6.5 (7, 7, 7.5, 7.5, 8, 8, 8.5, 8.5, 9, 9, 9.5)″
E 2.75 (3.25, 3.25, 3.25, 3.5, 4.25, 4.25, 4.5, 4.5, 4.75, 4.75, 4.75)″
F 8.5 (8, 9, 9, 9, 8.5, 8, 8, 8, 8, 7.5)″
G 1″
H 4″
I 9 (9.25, 10, 10.5, 10.75, 11.25, 12, 12.5, 12.75, 13.5, 14, 14.25)″

EASY LAYERING TANK

by Felecia O'Connell

FINISHED MEASUREMENTS

34.25 (36, 37.75, 40.5, 42.25, 44)" finished bust measurement; garment is meant to be worn with approximately 2" of positive ease.

YARN

Knit Picks Alpaca Cloud Lace (100% Baby Alpaca; 440 yards/50g): MC Catherine 26764, 2 (2, 2, 2, 3, 3) balls, C1 Beth 26765, 1 ball.

NEEDLES

US 8 (5mm) 24" circular needles, or size to obtain gauge

NOTIONS

Stitch Markers (optional)
Blocking wires or plenty of t-pins

GAUGE

18 sts and 24 rows = 4" over Stitch Pattern, blocked.

Easy Layering Tank

Notes:

This top is worked flat, in alternating rows of one and two strands of yarn. Before beginning, wind each skein into two balls of equal size.

All stitch counts include two selvedge stitches on each side of each piece. It may help to place a stitch marker following the first two selvedge stitches and immediately preceding the last two selvedge stitches.

Stitch Pattern (worked flat over an odd number of sts)

Row 1 (RS): With two strands held together, K1, P1, *K1, Sl 1 WYIF, repeat from * to last 3 sts, K1, P1, K1.
Row 2 (WS): With two strands held together, K1, P to last st, K1.
Row 3: With one strand of yarn, K1, P1, *Sl 1 WYIF, K1, rep to last 3 sts, Sl1 WYIF, P1, K1.
Row 4: With one strand of yarn, K1, P to last st, K1.
Rep Rows 1-4 for pattern.

Decreases

Wherever decreases are called for, work as follows: On RS row, K1, P1 (selvedge), SSK, work Stitch Pattern until last 4 sts, K2tog, P1, K1 (selvedge). 2 sts dec.

Bind Off

Bind off on WS using a Lace bind-off as follows: *K first 2 sts together TBL. Sl resulting st back onto LH needle, P-wise. Repeat from * until only one st remains. Cut yarn and pull it through that last st.

DIRECTIONS

Back

Lower Edge

With MC, using slipknot cast on, CO 87 (91, 95, 101, 105, 109) sts. Work Rows 1-4 of Stitch Pattern beginning with Row 3 and using two strands of yarn held together. Work next 2 rows of Stitch Pattern as established with one strand of yarn.

Body Decreases

Continue working Stitch Pattern from Row 31, decreasing 1 st on each side, every 21 rows, 3 times. 81 (85, 89, 95, 99, 103) sts. Continue to work even until piece measures 16 (16, 16.5, 16.5, 17, 17)" from CO edge ending with a WS row.

Raglan Shaping

BO 8 (9, 10, 11, 11, 12) sts at beginning of next 2 rows. 65 (67, 69, 73, 77, 79) sts.
Continue in Stitch Pattern, reestablishing selvedge sts on each side of piece, and decreasing 1 st on each side every RS row, 18 (18, 19, 20, 21, 21) times. 29 (31, 31, 33, 35, 37) sts.
Continue working straight if necessary, until piece measures 22.25 (22.25, 23, 23.25, 24.25, 24.25)" from CO edge. BO remaining sts.

Front

Work as for Back through Body Decreases. 81 (85, 89, 95, 99, 103) sts.
Continue to work even until piece measures 14.5 (14.5, 15, 15, 15.5, 15.5)" from CO edge.

Raglan Shaping

Work exactly as for Back until 29 (31, 31, 33, 35, 37) sts remain. Continue working straight if necessary, until piece measures 20.75 (20.75, 21.5, 21.75, 22.75, 22.75)" from CO edge ending on a RS row. BO all sts.

Sleeve Straps (make 2)

The sleeves are worked flat from the bottom (wider) edge up.

With 2 strands of C1, using slipknot cast on, CO 71 (71, 73, 73, 75, 75) sts.
Work Rows 1-2 of Stitch Pattern with two strands of yarn held together, then begin decreasing as follows:

Dec Row 1 (RS): K1, P1 (selvedge), SSK twice, work Stitch Pattern Row 3 until last 6 sts, K2tog twice, P1, K1. 4 sts dec, 67 (67, 69, 69, 71, 71) sts.
Row 2 (WS): K1, P1 (selvedge), P to last st, K1 .
Row 3: Repeat Dec Row 1, working Stitch Pattern Row 1. 4 sts dec, 63 (63, 65, 65, 67, 67) sts.

Decrease 1 st from each side of every RS row (2 sts dec per RS row) 9 times and work Stitch Pattern as established (this is a total decrease of 26 sts since CO, worked over 22 rows).
BO remaining 45 (45, 47, 47, 49, 49) sts.

Finishing

Weave in ends, wash and block each piece to diagram measurements.

Match short end of straps to top front neck edges. Using a yarn needle and C1, stitch straps to fronts. Match straps to neck edges of back and stitch straps to back.

Tack in the selvedge stitches at the armholes and along back hem to neaten edges and stabilize the garment.

Using a damp pressing cloth and an iron set to the lowest steam setting, lightly press the whole garment, remove the cloth, and allow garment to dry thoroughly prior to removing it from the blocking surface.

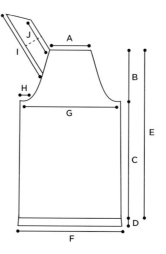

A 6.5 (7, 7, 7.25, 7.5, 8)"
B 6 (6, 6, 6.5, 7, 7)"
C 14.5 (14.5, 15, 15, 15.5, 15.5)"
D 1.5"
E 20.5 (20.5, 21, 21.5, 22.5, 22.5)"
F 19 (19.5, 20.5, 21.5, 22.5, 23.5)"
G 17 (18, 19, 20, 21, 22)"
H 2 (2, 2, 2.5, 2.5, 2.5)"
I 16 (16, 16.25, 17, 18, 18)"
J 10 (10, 11, 11, 11.5, 11.5)"

MAGNOLIA PULLOVER

by Allison Griffith

FINISHED MEASUREMENTS

34.75 (38.5, 42, 45.75, 49.5, 53, 56.75, 60.5, 64)" finished bust measurement; garment is meant to be worn with at least 4" of positive ease.

YARN

Knit Picks Stroll Sock Yarn (75% Superwash Merino Wool; 25% Nylon; 231 yards/50g): MC Wonderland Heather 25028, 3 (4, 4, 4, 5, 5, 6, 6, 7) balls.
Knit Picks Stroll Glimmer Yarn (70% Fine Superwash Merino Wool; 25% Nylon; 5% Stellina; 231 yards/50g): C1 Glimmer Frost 25495, 2 (2, 2, 3, 3, 3, 4, 4, 4) balls.

NEEDLES

US 6 (4mm) straight or circular needles, or size to obtain gauge
US 6 (4mm) DPNs or 16" circular needle, or size to obtain gauge
US 6 (4mm) 24" or longer circular needle, depending on size knit, or size to obtain gauge

NOTIONS

Stitch Markers
Scrap Yarn or Stitch Holder (optional)
Yarn Needle

GAUGE

20 sts and 32 rows = 4" over Magnolia Lace Chart, blocked.
24 sts and 34 rows = 4" in St st, blocked.

Magnolia Pullover

Notes:

The Magnolia Pullover is knit in pieces, then seamed. The back is worked in C1 Stroll Glimmer, while the rest of the sweater is worked in MC Stroll Sock. Once the Back, Front, and Sleeves are completed, the Front and Back are joined together at the shoulders. A narrow collar is then picked up and worked in the round. Sleeves are joined to the shoulders, and then the side/underarm sleeves are sewed closed. A ribbed bottom hem is then picked up and knit in the round.

The chart is read from right to left on RS rows (odd numbers) and left to right on WS rows (even numbers).

K2, P2 Rib (worked in the rnd over multiples of 4 sts)
All Rnds: *K2, P2; rep from * to end of rnd.

DIRECTIONS

Back

With C1, loosely CO 95 (105, 115, 125, 135, (145,) 155, 165, 175) sts. Prepare to work back and forth.

K 1 row (RS).

P 1 row (WS).

Work Magnolia Lace Chart rows 1-16 10 (10, 10, 11, 11, 11, 12, 12, 12) times, working the pattern repeat 7 (8, 9, 10, 11, 12, 13, 14, 15) times across each row. Finish with WS Row 16. 20.25 (20.25, 20.25, 22.25, 22.25, 22.25, 24.25, 24.25, 24.25)" from CO edge.

K 1 row.

P 1 row.

BO loosely.

Front   *SAME AS BACK CO. 145*

With MC, CO 55 (67, 79, 91, 101, 113, 125, 137, 149) sts. Prepare to work back and forth.

Work 4 (4, 4, 5, 5, 5, 6, 6, 6) rows in St st.

Increase Row: Work 2 sts in St st (K on RS, P on WS), inc 1 st, work in St st to 2 sts before end, inc 1 st, work 2 sts in St st. 2 sts inc.

Continue working an Increase Row every 5(5, 5, 6, 6, 6, 7, 7, 7)th row a total of 20 (19, 18, 17, 17, 16, 15, 14, 13) times. 95 (105, 115, 125, 135, 145, 155, 165, 175) sts remain.

Continue in St st (with no more shaping) until piece measures 18 (18, 18, 20, 20, 20, 22, 22, 22)" from edge, ending with a WS row.

Split for Neck

Next Row (RS): K 32 (36, 40, 44, 48, 52, 56, 60, 64), BO 31 (33, 35, 37, 39, 41, 43, 45, 47), K 32 (36, 40, 44, 48, 52, 56, 60, 64).

Right Shoulder

Continue only working sts for Right Shoulder. Leave the Left Shoulder sts on the needle or transfer to stitch holder.

Continue working in St st, decreasing every RS row along the neck edge as follows:

Dec 1 (RS): BO 3 sts, then K to end 1 (1, 1, 1, 1, 2, 2, 2, 2) time(s). 29 (33, 37, 41, 45, 46, 50, 54, 58) sts remain.

Dec 2 (RS): BO 2 sts, then K to end 1 (2, 2, 3, 3, 2, 2, 3, 3) time(s). 27 (29, 33, 35, 39, 42, 46, 48, 52) sts remain.

Dec 3 (RS): Dec 1, then K to end 2 times. 25 (27, 31, 33, 37, 40, 44, 46, 50) sts remain.

Work even in St st until piece measures 20.25 (20.25, 20.25, 22.25, 22.25, 22.25, 24.25, 24.25, 24.25)" from CO edge.

BO loosely.

Work Left Shoulder in the same way as Right Shoulder, reversing shaping.

Sleeves (Make 2)

With MC, CO 42 (46, 54, 58, 62, 66, 70, 78, 82) sts. Prepare to work back and forth.

Row 1: K2, (P2, K2) across.

Row 2: P2, (K2, P2) across.

Repeat Rows 1-2 8 (8, 8, 10, 10, 10, 12, 12, 12) more times.

Next Row: Knit, increasing 2 (4, 2, 4, 6, 8, 10, 8, 10) sts evenly across the row. 44 (50, 56, 62, 68, 74, 80, 86, 92) sts remain.

Work 5 rows in St st.

Increase Row: Work 2 sts in St st, inc 1 st, work in St st to 2 sts before end, inc 1 st, work 2 sts in St st. 2 sts inc.

Continue working sleeve in St st, working an Increase Row every 5th row a total of 21 (22, 21, 22, 23, 24, 25, 24, 25) times. 84 (90, 96, 102, 108, (114,) 120, 126, 132) sts remain.

Continue in St st (with no more shaping) until piece measures 17.5 (17.5, 17.5, 17.5, 17.5, 17, 17, 16, 15.5)" or desired length from edge, ending with a WS row.

BO loosely.

Finishing

Collar

Seam Front and Back together at shoulders. With MC and RS facing, PU 88 (100, 104, 116, 120 128, 132, 144, 148) sts around neckline. PM and prepare to work in the round.

Work K2, P2 Rib for 4 rounds.

BO loosely in pattern.

Assembly

Mark 13 (12.5, 12, 13.5, 13, 12.5, 14, 13.5, 13)" up from bottom edge of sweater. Sew sleeves above this into the sides of the sweater, centering the sleeves on the shoulder seam.

Sew body sides, sleeve seams and underarms together, being sure to match edges at cuffs, hem and underarm seams.

Hem

With MC and RS facing, PU 144 (168, 188, 212, 232, 252, 276, 296, 320) sts around bottom CO edge. PM and prepare to work in the round.

Work K2, P2 Rib for 2 (2.5, 3, 2, 2.5, 3, 2, 2.5, 3)".

BO loosely in pattern.

Weave in ends and block to diagram.

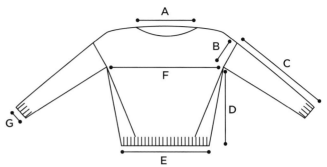

A 7.75 (8, 7.75, 8, 7.75, 7.75, 7.5, 7.75, 7.5)″
B 7 (7.5, 8, 8.5, 9, 9.5, 10, 10.5, 11)″
C 17.5 (17.5, 17.5, 17.5, 17.5, 17, 17, 16, 15.5)″
D 15 (15, 15, 15.5, 15.5, 15.5, 16, 16, 16)″
E 14 (16, 18, 20, 22, 24, 26, 28, 30)″
F 17.5 (19.25, 21, 23, 24.75, 26.5, 28.5, 30.25, 32)″
G 3.5 (3.75, 4.5, 4.75, 5.25, 5.5, 5.75, 6.5, 6.75)″

Magnolia Lace Chart

| | 35 | 34 | 33 | 32 | 31 | 30 | 29 | 28 | 27 | 26 | 25 | 24 | 23 | 22 | 21 | 20 | 19 | 18 | 17 | 16 | 15 | 14 | 13 | 12 | 11 | 10 | 9 | 8 | 7 | 6 | 5 | 4 | 3 | 2 |

(Magnolia Lace Chart grid, rows numbered 1–16, showing knit, k2tog, ssk, k3tog, and yo symbols; pattern repeat outlined from column 22 to column 13)

Legend

knit
RS: knit stitch
WS: purl stitch

k2tog
Knit two stitches together as one stitch

yo
yarn over

ssk
Slip one stitch as if to knit, slip another stitch as if to knit. Insert left-hand needle into front of these 2 stitches and knit them together

k3tog
Knit three stitches together as one

pattern repeat

VITTA COWL

by Angie Schwenn

FINISHED MEASUREMENTS

8" high x 60" circumference

YARN

Knit Picks Alpaca Cloud Lace (100% Baby Alpaca; 440 yards/50g): C1 Oyster Heather 24807, C2 Emma 26790, 1 ball each.

NEEDLES

US 6 (4mm) 24" or longer circular needles, or size to obtain gauge

NOTIONS

Yarn Needle
Stitch Marker

GAUGE

26 sts and 42 rounds = 4" over Stitch Pattern A, blocked.

Vitta Cowl

Notes:

The cowl is knit in the round lengthwise using two colors to create stripes of random, varying widths. A chart is included to guide the color changes. Follow all chart rows from right to left, reading them as RS rows.

Stitch Pattern A (in the round over an even number of sts)
Round 1: *P1, Sl 1 P-wise WYIF* repeat between * to end of round.
Round 2: Knit all sts.
Round 3: *Sl 1 P-wise WYIF, P1* repeat between * to end of round.
Round 4: Knit all sts.
Rep Rounds 1-4 for pattern.

DIRECTIONS

CO 390 sts, PM, join for working in the round being careful not to twist sts.

Next Round: Knit all sts. If working from chart, Round 1 of chart completed.

Work in Stitch Pattern A according to chart, repeating the chart row 39 times across the round. Between colors carry the yarn not being used loosely up the back of the work locking it into place each round with the working yarn, or break the yarn between colors. Work Chart Rows 1-83 once.

If following the Stitch Pattern A written instructions, repeat Rows 1-4 20 times, then Rows 1-2 once, changing colors as indicated on the chart.

BO all sts loosely.

Finishing

Weave in ends, wash, and block to size.

Legend

☐ **knit**
knit stitch

Ⅴ **slip wyif**
Slip stitch as if to purl, with yarn in front

• **purl**
purl stitch

Vitta Cowl Chart

TRAVERTINE

by Kirsten Singer

FINISHED MEASUREMENTS

25.5 (30.5, 36, 41.5, 46.5, 49.5, 54.5, 60, 65.5)" finished bust measurement; garment is meant to be worn with 0" of ease.

YARN

Knit Picks Lindy Chain (70% Linen, 30% Pima Cotton; 180 yards/50g): Whisper 26465, 3 (3, 4, 4, 5, 5, 6, 6, 7) skeins.

NEEDLES

US 6 (4.0mm) straight needles, or size to obtain gauge
US 6 (4.0mm) DPNs or two 24" circular needles for two circulars technique, or one 32" or longer circular needle for Magic Loop technique, or size to obtain gauge

NOTIONS

Yarn Needle
Scrap Yarn or Stitch Holder
Blocking Wires
Crochet Hook and Waste Yarn, or as preferred for Provisional CO

GAUGE

18 sts and 26 rows = 4" over Lace Pattern, blocked.

Travertine

Notes:

This unusual top is worked in four separate pieces: Right and Left Fronts, and Right and Left Backs. Each starts with a provisional cast on and is worked from the bottom up. Once the pieces are completed and blocked, you will join the two Fronts and two Backs together to create the wrap and then seam the side seams. Armholes have stitches picked up around to create a neat garter stitch finish.

Keep Lace Pattern even as you work Neck and Arm Decreases. If you do not have enough sts to complete a YO, K2tog, or SKP, YO pair, work the sts in St st (K on RS, P on WS).

Due to the nature of the lace pattern and the yarn, it is highly recommended to use blocking wires to shape garment to schematic measurements.

When removing provisional cast on, you will lose one stitch from initial cast on.

Lace Pattern (worked flat over multiples of 6 sts plus 3)
Rows 1, 3, and 5 (RS): K2, *YO, K2tog, K1, SKP, YO, K1; rep from * to last st, K1.
Row 2, 4, 6, 8, 10, 12 (WS): K1, P to last st, K1.
Rows 7, 9, and 11: K1 *SKP, YO, K1, YO, K2tog, K1; rep from * to last st, K1.
Rep Rows 1–12 for pattern.

Garter Stitch (worked in the round over any number of sts)
Rnd 1: Purl.
Rnd 2: Knit.
Rep Rnds 1-2 for pattern.

Three Needle Join
Hold the two pieces to be joined in your Left hand, with the RS facing you. Insert the RH needle into the first st of the piece on top as if to knit it, then insert the same needle into the first st of the piece on the bottom as if to knit it. Loop the yarn around the needle as if to knit, and pull the yarn between both sts as a K2tog and pull the sts off of the LH needle. Two sts have been joined together as one.

DIRECTIONS

Left Front and Right Back (make 2)
Using a provisional method, CO 57 (69, 81, 93, 105, 111, 123, 135, 147) sts.
Begin working Lace Pattern, and work even for 12 (12, 12, 12, 12, 12, 0, 0, 0) rows.

Neck and Armhole shaping occur at the same time, read through both instructions before proceeding.
Neck Shaping
Neck Decrease Row (RS): Work to last 4 sts, K2tog, K2. 1 st dec.
Work Neck Decrease Row every RS row 33 (45, 55, 59, 70, 75, 85, 90, 101) times.

Armhole Shaping
At the same time, when piece measures 14.5 (14.75, 15, 15.5, 15.75, 16, 17, 18, 20.5)" from CO edge, begin armhole shaping as follows:
BO 3 (3, 4, 4, 5, 5, 6, 6, 6) sts at the beginning of the next RS row.
BO 3 (3, 3, 4, 4, 4, 5, 6, 6) sts at the beginning of the next RS row.

Armhole Decrease Row (RS): K2, SKP, work to end. 1 st dec.
Work Armhole Decrease Row every RS row 3 (3, 4, 5, 5, 6, 6, 6, 7) times.

At the completion of all Neck and Armhole Shaping there will be 15 (15, 15, 21, 21, 21, 21, 27, 27) sts remaining.

Continue to work even in Lace Pattern until Armhole measures 6.25 (6.75, 7.5, 8.5, 9, 9.5, 10, 10.25, 10.75)" from Armhole bind offs, ending with a WS row.

BO all sts.

Right Front and Left Back (make 2)
Using a provisional method, CO 57 (69, 81, 93, 105, 111, 123, 135, 147) sts.
Begin working Lace Pattern, and work even for 12 (12, 12, 12, 12, 12, 0, 0, 0) rows.

Neck and Armhole shaping occur at the same time, read through both instructions before proceeding.
Neck Shaping
Neck Decrease Row (RS): K2, SKP, work to end. 1 st dec.
Work Neck Decrease Row every RS row 33 (45, 55, 59, 70, 75, 85, 90, 101) times.

Armhole Shaping
At the same time, when piece measures 14.5 (14.75, 15, 15.5, 15.75, 16, 17, 18, 20.5)" from CO edge, begin armhole shaping as follows:
BO 3 (3, 4, 4, 5, 5, 6, 6, 6) sts at the beginning of the next WS row.
BO 3 (3, 3, 4, 4, 4, 5, 6, 6) sts at the beginning of the next WS row.

Armhole Decrease Row (RS): Work to last 4 sts, K2tog, K2. 1 st dec.
Work Armhole Decrease Row every RS row 3 (3, 4, 5, 5, 6, 6, 6, 7) times.

At the completion of all Neck and Armhole Shaping there will be 15 (15, 15, 21, 21, 21, 21, 27, 27) sts remaining.

Continue to work even in Lace Pattern until Armhole measures 6.25 (6.75, 7.5, 8.5, 9, 9.5, 10, 10.25, 10.75)" from Armhole bind offs, ending with a WS row.

BO all sts.

Finishing
Weave in ends, and using blocking wires, block pieces according to diagram.

Body Join
Once blocked, join fronts and back as follows:
With RS of Right Front facing you, remove provisional CO and place these 56 (68, 80, 92, 104, 110, 122, 134, 146) sts on a straight

needle. With the RS of Left Front facing you, remove provisional CO and place these 56 (68, 80, 92, 104, 110, 122, 134, 146) sts on a straight needle. Work the Three Needle Join for Hem directions, below.

With RS of Right Back facing you, remove provisional CO and place 56 (68, 80, 92, 104, 110, 122, 134, 146) sts on a straight needle. With the RS of Left Back facing you, remove provisional CO and place these 56 (68, 80, 92, 104, 110, 122, 134, 146) sts on a straight needle. Work the Three Needle Join for Hem directions, below.

Three Needle Join for Hem
Overlap the Right Front over the Left Front with the RS of each piece facing you. Using a circular needle, K through both the first st of the Right Front and Left Front as a K2tog (you have now joined the first st of both fronts together, creating a new knit st on your circular needles). Continue across in this manner until all 56 (68, 80, 92, 104, 110, 122, 134, 146) sts have been zipped together and are on your RH needle.

After placing provisionally CO Right Back and Left Back sts on straight needles, overlap the Left Back over the Right Back with the RS of each piece facing you. Using the same circular needle, join the sts in the same manner until all 56 (68, 80, 92, 104, 110, 122, 134, 146) sts have been zipped together and are on your RH needle.

There are now 112 (136, 160, 184, 208, 220, 244, 268, 292) sts on your circular needle. PM to indicate the beginning of the rnd.

Hem
Work in Garter st for 5 rnds, ending with a Purl round.
BO all sts.
Seam sides and shoulder seams.

Armhole Edging
Using DPNs, PU and K 58 (61, 68, 76, 81, 85, 89, 92, 96) sts evenly around armhole opening (approximately 2 sts for every 3 rows). PM to indicate the beginning of the rnd.

Work in Garter st for 3 rounds, ending with a Purl round.
BO all sts.

Weave in all ends.

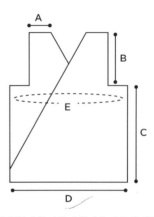

A 3.3 (3.3, 3.3, 4.5, 4.5, 4.5, 4.5, 6, 6)″
B 6.25 (6.75, 7.5, 8.5, 9, 9.5, 10, 10.25, 10.75)″
C 14.5 (14.75, 15, 15.5, 15.75, 16, 16.5, 17, 17.25)″
D 12.5 (15.5, 18, 20.5, 23, 24.5, 27.5, 30.5, 32.5)″
E 25 (31, 36, 41, 46, 49, 55, 61, 65)″

CHILLA

by Amanda Schwabe

FINISHED MEASUREMENTS

32 (36, 40, 44, 48, 52, 56, 60, 64)"
finished bust measurement; garment
is meant to be worn with 2" or less of
positive ease.

YARN

Knit Picks Galileo (50% Merino Wool, 50%
Viscose from Bamboo; 131 yards/50g):
MC Pearl 26103.

Sleeved Solid Version (pictured):
8 (8, 9, 11, 12, 13, 14, 15, 16) balls total
Sleeved Striped Version:
C1 Argent 26574, 4 (4, 5, 6, 6, 7, 7, 8, 8)
balls, C2 Comfrey 26577, 4 (4, 5, 6, 6, 7, 7,
8, 8) balls

Sleeveless Solid Version:
5 (6, 7, 7, 8, 9, 10, 10, 11) balls total

Sleeveless Striped Version:
C1 Argent 26574, 3 (3, 4, 4, 4, 5, 5, 5, 6)
balls, C2 Comfrey 26577, 3 (3, 4, 4, 4, 5, 5,
5, 6) balls

NEEDLES

US 5 (3.75mm) straight or circular
needles, or size to obtain gauge
US 4 (3.5mm) straight or circular needles,
or one size smaller than size used to
obtain gauge

NOTIONS

Five 0.5" Buttons
Yarn Needle
Stitch Markers

GAUGE

21 sts and 29 rows = 4" in St st on larger
needles, blocked.

Chilla

Notes:

Chilla is a cardigan that opens from the back with a subtle A-line shape; it is knit in pieces from the bottom up and then seamed. You can knit it with three-quarter length sleeves or as a sleeveless top. Either way, it's perfect for layering over your favorite shirts. It features a scoop neck in the front for a classic style, and it looks cute in a solid color or with narrow, two-row stripes.

The button holes are made with yarnovers and will fit small 0.5" buttons. They're worked in the top third of the sweater; the back is meant to hang open in the bottom two-thirds.

The hems are folded for neat, tailored edges, and the fold is accomplished by knitting, not sewing. Do not include the selvedge sts (1 at each side seam after the purl turning row) in the fold. You can use your regular cast on technique or a provisional cast on to get started. The hem is made by knitting about 0.75" in Stockinette st, then working a purl turning row so the hem will fold neatly towards the inside of the garment, then knitting another 0.75" of Stockinette. Then, you'll fold the hem up towards the WS and work 1 st from the needle together with 1 st from the cast-on edge, repeating that until the entire hem has been folded. You can always sew the hem up during the finishing process if you prefer, but I prefer to knit it in.

Once the hem has been folded, all measurements will be taken from the folded hem edge, not the CO that has now been folded up.

The public openings of the sweater (the cardigan openings in back, the arm holes on the sleeveless version) are worked with slipped-st edging, and the collar is picked up and knit from the neck edges.

The sweater is meant to be knit with 2" of positive ease. If your desired size falls between the given sizes, then one way to modify is to work the stitch instructions for the Front one size smaller, keeping the length instructions the same.

If you'd rather modify the sleeves to full length, cast on the same number as given for your size but spread the increases further apart, then work straight until your sleeve is the desired length.

If binding off on a knit row, BO in K. If binding off on a purl row, BO in P. Slip sts P-wise unless otherwise instructed.

Stockinette Stitch (St st, worked flat over any number of sts)
Row 1 (RS): K.
Row 2 (WS): P.
Rep Rows 1-2 for pattern.

Slipped-Stitch Edging (worked flat over any number of sts)
Row 1 (RS): Sl 1 P-wise WYIF, P1, work to last 2 sts, P1, K1.
Row 2 (WS): Sl 1 P-wise WYIF, K1, work to last 2 sts, K2.
Rep Rows 1-2 for pattern.

Two-Row Stripes (optional)
Work 2 rows in color C1.
Work 2 rows in color C2.

Continue alternating colors as established. Carry the unused color up the side, being careful not to pull the strands too tight and pucker the fabric.

Mattress Stitch
Sew the running stitches to each other, one full stitch in from each edge. A tutorial can be found at: http://tutorials.knitpicks.com/wptutorials/mattress-stitch/

DIRECTIONS

Front
Using smaller needles and MC, CO 95 (100, 111, 121, 132, 146, 150, 158, 168) sts.

Rows 1-6: Work in St st, beginning with a RS row.

Row 7 (RS): PFB, P to last st, PFB. 97 (102, 113, 123, 134, 148, 152, 160, 170) sts. Two selvedge sts have been added, 1 at each edge. This purl row is where the hem will fold neatly in half during Row 13.

Rows 8-12: Using larger needle, work 5 rows in St st.

Row 13 Hem-folding row (See Notes for more detail) (RS): K1, *K 1 st from needle together with 1 loop from CO edge; rep from * until 1 st remains on needle and all CO sts have been incorporated, K1. 97 (102, 113, 123, 134, 148, 152, 160, 170) sts.

Work in St st until piece measures 4 (4.25, 4.5, 4.5, 4.75, 4.75, 4.75, 5, 5.25)" from folding row, ending after a WS row.

Dec 2 sts every 12 (24, 26, 26, 26, 20, 38, 0, 0)th row 6 (3, 3, 3, 3, 4, 2, 0, 0) times as follows (RS): K1, K2tog, K until 3 sts remain, SSK, K1. 85 (96, 107, 117, 128, 138, 148, 160, 170) sts.

Work even until piece measures 15.75 (16.25, 16.75, 16.75, 16.75, 17, 17, 17.25, 17.25)" from folding row, ending after a WS row.

Shape Armholes and Neckline
We'll be shaping the armholes and neckline and shoulder at the same time, so make sure you read ahead during this section and refer to the diagram for a visual overview of what happens when.

Armhole Shaping
BO 2 (4, 7, 9, 12, 12, 12, 12, 12) sts at beginning of next 2 rows. 81 (88, 93, 99, 104, 114, 124, 136, 146) sts.

Sleeved Version: Dec 1 st at each Armhole edge every RS row 6 (7, 8, 10, 11, 15, 19, 23, 26) times as follows: K1, SSK, work pattern until 3 sts remain, K2tog, K1.
Work even until Shoulder Shaping.

Sleeveless Version: Decrease 1 st at each Armhole edge every RS row 6 (7, 8, 10, 11, 15, 19, 23, 26) times incorporating Slipped-Stitch Edging as follows:
RS: Sl 1 P-wise WYIF, P1, SSK, work in pattern until 4 sts remain, K2tog, P1, K1.
WS: Sl 1 P-wise WYIF, K1, P until 2 sts remain, K2.
Work even, continuing with Slipped-Stitch Edging (see Notes) as established until Shoulder Shaping.

Neckline Shaping
At the same time, when piece measures 0.25 (1, 1.5, 2, 2.5, 2.75, 3.25, 3.25, 3.75)" from beginning of armhole, work Neckline Shaping as follows:

Place a marker on either side of center 27 (28, 27, 27, 28, 26, 28, 28, 28) sts.

RS: Work Left shoulder as established to 1 st before 1st M, KFB, remove M, K1, pass newly-created st over the K st, BO to 2nd M, remove M, BO 1, work Right Shoulder as established to end. The Left Shoulder sts will now be ignored while the Right Shoulder is finished; you can leave them on the needle until it's time to work them. Make a note of where you left off in the Armhole Shaping so you can resume the decreases later.

Next and Following WS Neckline Shaping Rows: Work Right Armhole Shaping as established until 1 st remains at neck edge, Sl 1.

Dec Row 1 (RS): Sl 2, PSSO, BO 2, work shoulder as established to end. 3 sts dec.

Dec Row 2 (RS): Sl 2, PSSO, BO 1, work shoulder as established to end. 2 sts dec.

Repeat Dec Row 2 once more.

Dec Row 3 (RS): Sl 2, PSSO, work shoulder as established to end. 1 st dec.

Repeat Dec Row 3 5 times more.

Work Neckline edge even, continuing with armhole decreases as established if necessary for your size.

Shoulder Shaping

At the same time, when piece measures 5.25 (6, 6.25, 6.5, 7, 7.25, 7.5, 7.5, 8)" from beginning of armhole after a RS row, work Shoulder Shaping as follows:

32" size only: 8 sts remain. BO 2 sts at beginning of every WS row 4 times.

36" size only: 10 sts remain. BO 2 sts at beginning of every WS row 5 times.

40" size only: 12 sts remain. BO 2 sts at beginning of every WS row 3 times, then BO 3 sts at beginning of every WS row twice.

44" size only: 13 sts remain. BO 2 sts at beginning of every WS row twice, then BO 3 sts at beginning of every WS row 3 times.

48" size only: 14 sts remain. BO 2 sts at beginning of every WS row 4 times, then BO 3 sts at beginning of every WS row twice.

52" and 56" sizes only: 16 sts remain. BO 2 sts at beginning of every WS row twice, then BO 3 sts at beginning of every WS row 4 times.

60" size only: 18 sts remain. BO 3 sts at beginning of every WS row 6 times.

64" size only: 20 sts remain. BO 2 sts at beginning of WS row once, then BO 3 sts at beginning of every WS row 6 times.

Left Shoulder

Join yarn at Neckline Edge, leaving a 6" tail, and purl one row (WS), working Armhole Shaping as established.

Next and Following RS Neckline Shaping Rows: Work Left Armhole Shaping as established until 1 st remains at neck edge, Sl 1.

Dec Row 1 (WS): Sl 2, PSSO, BO 2, work shoulder as established to end. 3 sts dec.

Dec Row 2 (WS): Sl 2, PSSO, BO 1, work shoulder as established to end. 2 sts dec.

Repeat Row 2 once more.

Dec Row 3 (WS): Sl 2, PSSO, work shoulder as established to end. 1 st dec.

Repeat Dec Row 3 five times more. 8 (10, 12, 13, 14, 16, 16, 18, 20) sts.

Work Neckline edge even, continuing with Armhole decreases as established if necessary for your size.

Shoulder Shaping

At the same time, when piece measures 5.25 (6, 6.25, 6.5, 7, 7.25, 7.5, 7.5, 8)" from beginning of armhole after a WS row, work Shoulder Shaping as follows:

32" size only: 8 sts remain. BO 2 sts at beginning of every RS row 4 times.

36" size only: 10 sts remain. BO 2 sts at beginning of every RS row 5 times.

40" size only: 12 sts remain. BO 2 sts at beginning of every RS row 3 times, then BO 3 sts at beginning of every RS row twice.

44" size only: 13 sts remain. BO 2 sts at beginning of every RS row twice, then BO 3 sts at beginning of every RS row 3 times.

48" size only: 14 sts remain. BO 2 sts at beginning of every RS row 4 times, then BO 3 sts at beginning of every RS row twice.

52" and 56" sizes only: 16 sts remain. BO 2 sts at beginning of every RS row twice, then BO 3 sts at beginning of every RS row 4 times.

60" size only: 18 sts remain. BO 3 sts at beginning of every RS row 6 times.

64" size only: 20 sts remain. BO 2 sts at beginning of RS row once, then BO 3 sts at beginning of every RS row 6 times.

Back Right

The buttons will be sewn onto the left edge of this half during Finishing.

Using smaller needles and MC, CO 48 (50, 56, 61, 66, 73, 75, 79, 84) sts.

Rows 1-6: Work in St st, beginning with a RS row.

Row 7 (RS): PFB, P to end. 49 (51, 57, 62, 67, 74, 76, 80, 85) sts. One selvedge st has been added to the right edge. This purl row is where the hem will fold neatly in half during Row 13.

From now on, work Slipped-Stitch Edging at left edge only as follows:
RS: Work in pattern to last 2 sts, P1, K1.
WS: Sl 1 P-wise WYIF, K1, work in pattern to end.
The right (armhole) edge is where the selvedge st lives and where all the shaping will take place.

Rows 8-12: Using larger needles, work 5 rows in St st, working Slipped-Stitch Edging at left edge only.

Row 13 Hem-folding row (RS): K1, *K 1 st from needle together with 1 loop from CO edge; rep from * to end. All CO sts have been incorporated. 49 (51, 57, 62, 67, 74, 76, 80, 85) sts.

Work in St st until piece measures 4 (4.25, 4.5, 4.5, 4.75, 4.75, 4.75, 5, 5.25)" from edge, ending after a WS row.

Dec 1 st every 12 (24, 26, 26, 26, 20, 38, 0, 0)th row 6 (3, 3, 3, 3, 4, 2, 0, 0) times as follows (RS): K1, K2tog, K to last 2 sts, work Slipped-St Edging. 43 (48, 54, 59, 64, 70, 74, 80, 85) sts remain.

Work even until piece measures 15.75 (16.25, 16.75, 16.75, 16.75, 17, 17, 17.25, 17.25)" from bottom edge, ending after a WS row.

Armhole and Neckline shaping occur at the same time, read through both sections before proceeding.

Shape Armhole

Next RS Row: BO 2 (4, 7, 9, 12, 12, 12, 12, 12) sts, work in pattern to end. 41 (44, 47, 50, 52, 58, 62, 68, 73) sts.

Sleeved Version: Dec 1 st at Armhole edge every RS row 6 (7, 8, 10, 11, 15, 19, 23, 26) times as follows: K1, SSK, work in pattern to end.
Work even until Shoulder Shaping.

Sleeveless Version: Dec 1 st at Armhole edge every RS row 6 (7, 8, 10, 11, 15, 19, 23, 26) times, incorporating Slipped-Stitch Edging as follows:
RS: Sl 1 P-wise WYIF, P1, SSK, work in pattern to end.
WS: Work in pattern until 2 sts remain, K2.
Work even, continuing with Slipped-Stitch Edging as established until Neckline and Shoulder Shaping. 35 (37, 39, 40, 41, 43, 43, 45, 47) sts.

Neckline Shaping

At the same time, begin Neckline Shaping when piece measures 5.25 (6, 6.5, 7, 7.5, 7.75, 8.25, 8.25, 8.75)" from Armhole BO, ending after a RS row as follows:
All Sizes (WS): BO 25 sts, work in pattern to end.
Next Row (RS): Work in pattern to last st, Sl 1.
Next Row (WS): Sl 2, PSSO, work in pattern to end. 1 st dec.
Work last 2 rows once more. 8 (10, 12, 13, 14, 16, 16, 18, 20) sts.
Work Neckline edge even.

Shoulder Shaping

At the same time, begin Shoulder Shaping when piece measures 5.25 (6, 6.25, 6.5, 7, 7.25, 7.5, 7.5, 8)" from beg of armhole after a WS row as follows:
32" size only: 8 sts remain. BO 2 sts at beginning of every RS row 4 times.
36" size only: 10 sts remain. BO 2 sts at beginning of every RS row 5 times.
40" size only: 12 sts remain. BO 2 sts at beginning of every RS row 3 times, then BO 3 sts at beg of every RS row twice.
44" size only: 13 sts remain. BO 2 sts at beginning of every RS row twice, then BO 3 sts at beginning of every RS row 3 times.
48" size only: 14 sts remain. BO 2 sts at beginning of every RS row 4 times, then BO 3 sts at beginning of every RS row twice.
52" and 56" sizes only: 16 sts remain. BO 2 sts at beginning of every RS row twice, then BO 3 sts at beginning of every RS row 4 times.
60" size only: 18 sts remain. BO 3 sts at beginning of every RS row 6 times.
64" size only: 20 sts remain. BO 2 sts at beginning of RS row once, then BO 3 sts at beg of every RS row 6 times.

Back Left

This half of the cardigan is slightly wider than the Back Right to allow for a band of button holes, worked as part of the fabric and starting about two-thirds of the way up the back. There will be 5 buttonholes spaced just under 2" apart. There will be a couple things happening at the same time, so be sure to read ahead and check the diagram to get a good overview.

Using smaller needles and MC, CO 54 (56, 62, 67, 72, 79, 81, 85, 90) sts.

Rows 1-6: Work in St st, beginning with a RS row.

Row 7 (RS): P until 1 st remains, PFB. 55 (57, 63, 68, 73, 80, 82, 86, 91) sts. One selvedge st has been added to the left edge. This purl row is where the hem will fold neatly in half during Row 13.

From now on, work Slipped-Stitch Edging at right edge as follows:
RS: Sl 1 P-wise WYIF, P1, work in pattern to end.
WS: Work in pattern to last 2 sts, K2.
The left (armhole) edge is where the selvedge st lives and where all the shaping will take place.

Rows 8-12: Using larger needle, work 5 rows in St st, working Slipped-Stitch Edging at right edge only.
Row 13 Hem-folding row (WS): *K 1 st from needle together with 1 loop from CO edge; rep from * to last st, K1. All CO sts have been incorporated. 55 (57, 63, 68, 73, 80, 82, 86, 91) sts.

Work in St st until piece measures 4 (4.25, 4.5, 4.5, 4.75, 4.75, 4.75, 5, 5.25)" from edge, ending after a WS row.

Body decreases and Buttonholes are worked at the same time, read through both sections before proceeding.
Decrease 1 st every 12 (24, 26, 26, 26, 20, 38, 0, 0)th row 6 (3, 3, 3, 3, 4, 2, 0, 0) times as follows (RS): Work Slipped-St Edging, K to last 3 sts, SSK, K1. 49 (54, 60, 65, 70, 76, 80, 86, 91) sts.

Buttonholes

At the same time, when piece measures 13 (14.25, 15.25, 15.75, 16.25, 16.75, 17.25, 17.5, 18)" from bottom edge, work a buttonhole row on the RS as follows:
Sl 1 P-wise WYIF, P1, K2, YO, K2tog, work in pattern to end.
Repeat buttonhole row every 14th row 4 more times, for a total of 5 buttonholes.

At the same time, work even until piece measures 15.75 (16.25, 16.75, 16.75, 16.75, 17, 17, 17.25, 17.25)" from bottom edge, ending after a RS row.

Armhole and Neckline Shaping occur at the same time, read through both sections before proceeding.

Shape Armhole

Next WS Row: BO 2 (4, 7, 9, 12, 12, 12, 12, 12) sts, work in pattern to end.

Sleeved Version: Dec 1 st at Armhole edge every RS row 6 (7, 8, 10, 11, 15, 19, 23, 26) times as follows: Work in pattern to last 3 sts, K2tog, K1.
Work even until Shoulder Shaping.

Sleeveless Version: Dec 1 st at Armhole edge every RS row 6 (7, 8, 10, 11, 15, 19, 23, 26) times, incorporating Slipped-Stitch Edging as follows:
RS: Work in pattern to last 4 sts, K2tog, P1, K1.
WS: Sl 1 P-wise WYIF, K1, work in pattern to end.
Work even, continuing with Slipped-Stitch Edging as established until Neckline and Shoulder Shaping. 41 (43, 45, 46, 47, 49, 49, 51, 53) sts.

At the same time, begin Neckline Shaping when piece measures 5.25 (6, 6.5, 7, 7.5, 7.75, 8.25, 8.25, 8.75)" from Armhole BO, ending after a WS row as follows:

All Sizes (RS): BO 31 sts, work in pattern to end.

Next Row (WS): Work in pattern to last st, Sl 1.

Next Row (RS): Sl 2, PSSO, work in pattern to end. 1 st dec.
Work last 2 rows once more. 8 (10, 12, 13, 14, 16, 16, 18, 20) sts.
Work Neckline edge even.

At the same time, begin Shoulder Shaping when piece measures 5.25 (6, 6.25, 6.5, 7, 7.25, 7.5, 7.5, 8)" from beginning of Armhole BO after a RS row as follows:

32" size only: 8 sts remain. BO 2 sts at beginning of every WS row 4 times.

36" size only: 10 sts remain. BO 2 sts at beginning of every WS row 5 times.

40" size only: 12 sts remain. BO 2 sts at beginning of every WS row 3 times, then BO 3 sts at beginning of every WS row twice.

44" size only: 13 sts remain. BO 2 sts at beginning of every WS row twice, then BO 3 sts at beg of every WS row 3 times.

48" size only: 14 sts remain. BO 2 sts at beginning of every WS row 4 times, then BO 3 sts at beginning of every WS row twice.

52" and 56" sizes only: 16 sts remain. BO 2 sts at beginning of every WS row twice, then BO 3 sts at beginning of every WS row 4 times.

60" size only: 18 sts remain. BO 3 sts at beginning of every WS row 6 times.

64" size only: 20 sts remain. BO 2 sts at beginning of WS row once, then BO 3 sts at beginning of every WS row 6 times.

Sleeves (Optional, make 2)

The sleeves are worked flat from the wrists up.

Using smaller needles and MC, CO 42 (45, 48, 53, 57, 62, 64, 66, 66) sts.

Rows 1-6: Work in St st, beginning with a RS row.

Row 7 (RS): PFB, P to last st, PFB. 44 (47, 50, 55, 59, 64, 66, 68, 68) sts. Two selvedge sts have been added, 1 at each edge. This purl row is where the hem will fold neatly in half during Row 13.

Rows 8-12: Using larger needles, work 5 rows in St st.

Row 13 Hem-folding Row (RS): K1, *K 1 st from needle together with 1 loop from CO edge; rep from * until 1 st remains on needle and all CO sts have been incorporated, K1. 44 (47, 50, 55, 59, 64, 66, 68, 68) sts.

Increase 2 sts every 8 (8, 8, 8, 6, 6, 6, 6, 4)th row 5 (4, 5, 8, 11, 12, 12, 16, 18) times as follows: K1, M1L, K to last st, M1R, K1. 54 (55, 60, 71, 81, 88, 90, 100, 104) sts.

Work even until sleeve measures 12.5 (12.75, 12.75, 13, 13, 13.5, 13.5, 14, 14)" or desired length from Hem folding row.

Shape Sleeve Cap

BO 2 (4, 7, 9, 12, 12, 12, 12, 12) sts at beginning of next 2 rows. 50 (47, 46, 53, 57, 64, 66, 76, 80) sts.
Decrease 2 sts every RS row 12 (13, 14, 15, 16, 19, 19, 21, 22) times as follows: K1, SSK, K until 3 sts remain, K2tog, K1. 26 (21, 18, 23, 25, 26, 28, 34, 36) sts.
BO 2 sts at beginning of next 2 rows.

BO 4 sts at beginning of next 2 rows.
BO remaining 14 (9, 6, 11, 13, 14, 16, 22, 24) sts.

Finishing

Weave in ends. Wash and block to diagram. Allow to dry completely.

Use Mattress Stitch to sew sweater seams.
Sew shoulder seams.

Collar

Beginning at edge of cardigan opening on the Back Left (above the buttonholes), PU and K sts around the neckline for the collar, knitting them as you pick them up.

When picking up and knitting at the tops of columns, PU and K 1 st in each column. (This includes around the bias cast-off that forms the curves. Don't pick up in the spaces or gaps. Pick up directly in the top st of each column below the BO. It may look like you're not picking up enough on the slopes, but it will pull in the fabric at just the right rate to make a beautiful collar.)

When picking up and knitting at the edge of rows, PU and K at a rate of 3:4 (in each of 3 rows, then skipping the 4th).

Once all sts have been picked up and knit at the proper rate, count them. To work the 2x2 Ribbed collar, you'll need a multiple of 4 sts plus 2. If you can divide the number by 4 and have the answer end in .5, it will work as is. (For example, 82 / 4 = 20.5, which is perfect.) If you can't, then you'll need to decrease a st or two in ribbing during the first row to achieve a workable number of sts. I like to hide my decreases in a P section by working (P2tog, P1) instead of P2.

Row 1 (WS): Sl 1 P-wise WYIF, P1, *K2, P2; rep from * to end.

Row 2 (RS): Sl 1 P-wise WYIF, K1, *P2, K2; rep from * to end.
Repeat Rows 1-2 twice more, making a buttonhole in Row 4 (RS) as follows: Sl 1 P-wise WYIF, K1, P2, YO, K2tog, *P2, K2; rep from * to end.
BO in pattern.

Sew in sleeves.
Sew sleeve seams.
Sew side seams.
Align buttons with buttonholes and mark their place on the Back Right edge. Sew buttons in place.
Weave in remaining ends.

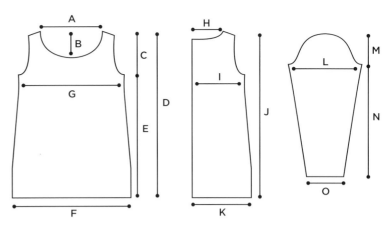

A 10"
B 6"
C 5.25 (5.75, 6.25, 6.75, 7, 7.25, 7.75, 7.5, 8.25)"
D 22 (23.25, 24.25, 24.75, 25.25, 25.75, 26.25, 26.5, 27)"
E 15.75 (16.25, 16.75, 16.75, 16.75, 17, 17, 17.25, 17.25)"
F 18 (19, 21, 23, 25, 27.5, 28.5, 30, 32)"
G 16 (18, 20, 22, 24, 26, 28, 30, 32)"
H 16 (18, 20, 22, 24, 26, 28, 30, 32)"
I 16 (18, 20, 22, 24, 26, 28, 30, 32)"
J 16 (18, 20, 22, 24, 26, 28, 30, 32)"
K 16 (18, 20, 22, 24, 26, 28, 30, 32)"
L 10 (10, 11, 13.25, 15, 16.25, 16.75, 18.75, 19.5)"
M 4.25 (4.5, 4.75, 5, 5.25, 6, 6, 6.5, 7)"
N 12.5 (12.75, 12.75, 13, 13, 13.5, 13.5, 14, 14)"
O 8 (8.75, 9.25, 10.25, 11, 11.75, 12.25, 12.75, 12.75)"

CATAMARAN

by Bekah Knits

FINISHED MEASUREMENTS

12 (20)" depth x 40 (63)"wide at widest point

YARN

Knit Picks Lindy Chain (70% Linen, 30% Pima Cotton; 180 yards/50g): C1 Silver 26453, C2 Ash 26449, 1 (2) balls.

NEEDLES

US 4 (3.5mm) 40" circular needle, or size to obtain gauge

NOTIONS

Yarn Needle

GAUGE

28 sts and 48 rows = 4" in St st, blocked.

Catamaran

Notes:

This stunning shawl is knit from the corner up and takes on its asymmetrical shape by a RS decrease and a WS double increase. The integrated i-cord edging and shawl shaping are all worked in the first 5 sts of every row.

A note on sizing

Because of the asymmetrical shape, the smaller shawl size does not have tails long enough to drape around the wearer's neck. They will need to be tucked under the shawl.

2yo (Double Yarn Over): YO two times. When working a double YO on the following row, on RS: (P1, K1), on WS: (K1, P1).

Carrying the yarn

For tidy edges, follow these rules:

When switching from C1 to C2 or likewise, place the live yarn over the top of the new yarn. To carry the yarn up the edge and avoid unnecessary ends, at the end of each WS row, put the live yarn under the inactive yarn so it is wrapped and carried up the knitting.

I-cord Bind Off

K2, K2tog TBL, Sl 3 sts back to left needle rep between * to last 6 sts. (Work in pattern across 2yo, knitting each yo TBL.) Sl 1 K-wise, K3tog, PSSO. K3tog, pull strand through final st and tighten.

DIRECTIONS

Set-Up Rows

CO 6 sts with C1.

Row 1 (RS): K3, WYIF Sl 3 P-wise.

Row 2 (WS): K3, WYIF Sl 3 P-wise.

Row 3: K3, WYIF Sl 3 P-wise.

Row 4: K3, M1L, WYIF Sl 3 P-wise. 7 sts.

Row 5: K3, KFB, WYIF Sl 3 P-wise. 8 sts.

Row 6: K3, KFB, K1, WYIF Sl 3 P-wise. 9 sts.

Row 7: K3, SSK, K1, WYIF Sl 3 P-wise. 8 sts.

Row 8: K3, 2yo, P2, WYIF Sl 3 P-wise. 10 sts.

Row 9: K3, SSK, K to last 5 sts (working 2yo as described in Pattern notes), WYIF Sl 3 P-wise. 1 st dec.

Row 10: K3, 2yo, P to last 3 sts, WYIF Sl 3 P-wise. 2 sts inc.

Repeat Rows 9 & 10 until there are 24 sts total (including the 2yo), ending with a WS (even) row.

Continue with C1. Begin written instructions below, or start at Row 1 of Lace Chart.

Lace Pattern

Row 1 (RS): K3, SSK, K1, *2yo, SKP, K2tog* rep to last 6 sts, K1, work 2yo as (P1, K1), WYIF Sl 3 P-wise.

Row 2 (and all even rows through 18) (WS): K3, 2yo, P across back working 2yo as (K1, P1) to last 3 sts, WYIF Sl 3 P-wise.

Row 3: K3, SSK, K1, *K2tog, 2yo, SKP* rep to last 7 sts, K2, (P1, K1), WYIF Sl 3 P-wise.

Row 5: K3, SSK, YO, SKP, *K2tog, 2yo, SKP* rep to last 7 sts, K2, (P1, K1), WYIF Sl 3 P-wise.

Row 7: K3, SSK, K1, *2yo, SKP, K2tog* rep to last 5 sts, (P1, K1), WYIF Sl 3 P-wise.

Row 9: K3, SSK, K1, *K2tog, 2yo, SKP* rep to last 6 sts, K1, (P1, K1), WYIF Sl 3 P-wise.

Row 11: K3, SSK, YO, SKP, *K2tog, 2yo, SKP* rep to last 6 sts, (P1, K1), WYIF Sl 3 P-wise.

Row 13: K3, SSK, K1, YO, SKP, *K2tog, 2yo, SKP* rep to last 6 sts, K1, (P1, K1), WYIF Sl 3 P-wise.

Row 15: K3, SSK, *K2tog, 2yo, SKP* rep to last 6 sts, K1, (P1, K1), WYIF Sl 3 P-wise.

Row 17: K3, SSK, K1, *K2tog, 2yo, SKP* rep to last 6 sts, K1, (P1, K1), WYIF Sl 3 P-wise.

Complete the lace section by ending on a WS Row 18. 9 sts inc.

Begin written instructions below, or start at Row 1 of Striping Chart.

Row 1 (RS): With C1, K3, SSK, K to last 5 sts, work 2yo as (P1, K1), WYIF Sl 3 P-wise.

Row 2 (WS): K3, 2yo, P to last 3 sts, WYIF Sl 3 P-wise.

Row 3: Rep Row 1.

Row 4: Rep Row 2.

Row 5: Change to C2, rep Row 1.

Row 6: Rep Row 2.

Row 7: Change to C1, rep Row 1.

Row 8: Rep Row 2.

Row 9-16: Rep Rows 5-8 2 more times.

Row 17: Change to C2, rep Row 1.

Row 18: Rep Row 2.

Rows 19-22: Rep Rows 1-2.

11 sts inc.

Rep Lace Pattern and Striping Pattern again, but this time invert the colors. For C1 use C2, and likewise.

Continue as established, working the Lace Pattern and Striping Pattern as written and then inverting the colors and rep again for a total of 3 (5) times. 84 (124) sts.

BO all sts in i-cord bind off.

Finishing

Weave in ends, wash and block to size.

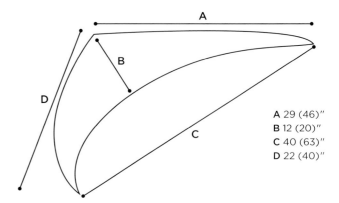

A 29 (46)"
B 12 (20)"
C 40 (63)"
D 22 (40)"

Lace Chart

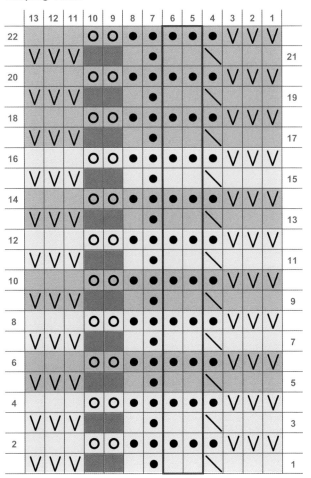

Note: In order for the chart to visually show the shaping of the shawl, extra repeats are shown (outlined in blue dashes).

Striping Chart

Legend

knit
knit stitch on RS and WS

ssk
Slip one stitch as if to knit, slip another stitch as if to knit. Insert left-hand needle into front of these 2 stitches and knit them together

purl
purl stitch on RS and WS

no stitch
placeholder - No stitch made.

slip
Slip stitch as if to purl, holding yarn in front

yo
yarn over

C1

C2

pattern repeat

SKP
slip 1, knit 1, pass slipped stitch over knit st

k2tog
Knit two stitches together as one stitch

RIPPLING TOP

by Quenna Lee

FINISHED MEASUREMENTS

32.75 (34.75, 36.75, 40, 42.75, 46.75, 51.25, 55.75, 59.75)" finished bust measurement; garment is meant to be worn with 1-3" of positive ease.

YARN

Knit Picks Galileo (50% Merino Wool, 50% Viscose from Bamboo; 131 yards/50g): White 26094, 7 (7, 7, 8, 9, 9, 10, 11, 12) balls.

NEEDLES

US 6 (4mm) 24" or longer circular needles depending on garment size plus spare DPN, or size to obtain gauge
US 5 (3.75mm) 16" circular needle, or 1 size smaller than needle to obtain gauge

NOTIONS

Yarn Needle
Stitch Markers
Scrap Yarn or Stitch Holder

GAUGE

24 sts and 30 rnds = 4" in St st in the round on larger needles, blocked.
Chart A (16 sts) = 2.75" wide on larger needles, blocked.
Chart B (21 sts) = 3.75" wide on larger needles, blocked.
Chart C (32 sts) = 5" wide on larger needles, blocked.

Rippling Top

Notes:

Rippling is an easy fitting top without waist shaping and minimal armhole shaping. It has an asymmetrical lace panel on the right side of the front and back. The lace panels are different according to size chosen.

Top is worked in the round in one piece to the armholes. Stitches are BO at the armholes and then the front and back are worked back and forth separately. The cap sleeves are formed with increases at the armhole edges.

There are two sets of short rows: the first to shape the sleeve cap, followed by one for the shoulders. The shoulders are seamed with a 3-Needle BO. The neckline is finished with a 1x1 ribbing.

The eyelet lace pattern can be worked with text or charts.

Working with lace chart patterns: To maintain a consistent stitch count, each YO must be paired with its decrease (K2TOG or SSK). If a pair is not complete (an odd number in the eyelet section), substitute with St st. When working in the rnd, read all chart rows from right to left as if a RS row. When working flat, read RS rows (odd numbers) from right to left, and WS rows (even numbers) from left to right.

Chart A (worked in the round over an multiple of 16 sts)
Rnd 1: P1, (YO, SSK) twice, P1, K1, P1, (YO, SSK) 3x, P1, K1.
Rnd 2: P1, K4, P1, K1, P1, K6, P1, K1.
Rnd 3: P1, (K2TOG, YO) twice, P1, K1, P1, (K2TOG, YO) 3x, P1, K1.
Rnd 4: Rep Rnd 2.
Rep Rnds 1-4 for pat.
To work Chart A back and forth, work as in the rnd, but even (WS) Rows: P1, K1, P6, K1, P1, K1, P4, K1.

Chart B (worked in the round over multiples of 21 sts)
Rnd 1: P1, (YO, SSK, P1, K1, P1, YO, SSK) twice, (YO, SSK) twice, P1, K1.
Rnd 2: P1, K2, P1, K1, P1, K4, P1, K1, P1, K6, P1, K1.
Rnd 3: P1, (K2TOG, YO, P1, K1, P1, K2TOG, YO) twice, (K2TOG, YO) twice, P1, K1
Rnd 4: Rep Rnd 2.
Rep Rnds 1-4 for pat.
To work Chart B back and forth, work as in the rnd, but even (WS) Rows: P1, K1, P6, K1, P1, K1, P4, K1, P1, K1, P2, K1.

Chart C (worked in the round over multiples of 32 sts)
Rnd 1: P1, YO, SSK, P1, K1, P1, *(YO, SSK) twice, P1, K1, P1, YO, SSK; rep from * once more, (YO, SSK) 3x, P1, K1.
Rnd 2: P1, K2, P1, K1, P1, K4, P1, K1, P1, K6, P1, K1, P1, K8, P1, K1.
Rnd 3: P1, K2TOG, YO, P1, K1, P1, *(K2TOG, YO) twice, P1, K1, P1, K2TOG, YO; rep from * once more, (K2TOG, YO) 3x, P1, K1.
Rnd 4: Rep Rnd 2.
Rep Rnds 1-4 for pat.
To work Chart C back and forth, work as in the rnd, but even (WS) Rows: P1, K1, P8, K1, P1, K1, P6, K1, P1, K1, P4, K1, P1, K1, P2, K1.

Chart D (worked in the round over an multiple of 16 sts)
Rnd 1: K1, P1, (YO, SSK) 3x, P1, K1, P1, (YO, SSK) twice, P1.
Rnd 2: K1, P1, K6, P1, K1, P1, K4, P1.

Rnd 3: K1, P1, (K2TOG, YO) 3x, P1, K1, P1, (K2TOG, YO) twice, P1.
Rnd 4: Rep Rnd 2.
Rep Rnds 1-4 for pat.
To work Chart D back and forth, work as in the rnd, but even (WS) Rows: K1, P4, K1, P1, K1, P6, K1, P1.

Chart E (worked in the round over an multiple of 21 sts)
Rnd 1: K1, P1, YO, SSK, *(YO, SSK) twice, P1, K1, P1; rep from * once more, YO, SSK, P1.
Rnd 2: K1, P1, K6, P1, K1, P1, K4, P1, K1, P1, K2, P1.
Rnd 3: K1, P1, K2TOG, YO, *(K2TOG, YO) twice, P1, K1, P1; rep from * once more, K2TOG, YO, P1.
Rnd 4: Rep Rnd 2.
Rep Rnds 1-4 for pat.
To work Chart E back and forth, work as in the rnd, but even (WS) Rows: K1, P2, K1, P1, K1, P4, K1, P1, K1, P6, K1, P1.

Chart F (worked in the round over an multiple of 32 sts)
Rnd 1: K1, P1, YO, SSK, *(YO, SSK) 3x, P1, K1, P1; rep from * once more, (YO, SSK) twice, P1, K1, P1, YO, SSK, P1.
Rnd 2: K1, P1, K8, P1, K1, P1, K6, P1, K1, P1, K4, P1, K1, P1, K2, P1.
Rnd 3: K1, P1, K2TOG, YO, *(K2TOG, YO) 3x, P1, K1, P1; rep from * once more, (K2TOG, YO) twice, P1, K1, P1, K2TOG, YO, P1.
Rnd 4: Rep Rnd 2.
Rep Rnds 1-4 for pat.
To work Chart F back and forth, work as in the rnd but even (WS) Rows: K1, P2, K1, P1, K1, P4, K1, P1, K1, P6, K1, P1, K1, P8, K1, P1.

1x1 Rib (worked in the rnd over an even number of sts)
All Rnds: *K1, P1; rep from * to end of rnd.

Garter st (in the round over any number of sts)
Rnd 1: Knit.
Rnd 2: Purl.
Rep Rnds 1-2 for pat.

Garter st (worked flat over any number of sts)
Knit every row.

Stockinette st (St st, worked flat over any number of sts)
Row 1: Knit.
Row 2: Purl.
Rep Rows 1-2 for pat.
To work St st in the rnd, K every rnd.

3-Needle Bind Off: *Hold the two pieces of knitting together with the points facing to the right. Insert a third needle into the first st on each of the needles K-wise, starting with the front needle. Work a K st, pulling the loop through both of the sts you've inserted the third needle through. After pulling the loop through, slip the first st off of each of the needles. Repeat from *. Pass the first finished st over the second and off of the needle.

Wrap and Turn (W&T): Tutorial on Knit Picks website can be found at http://tutorials.knitpicks.com/wptutorials/short-rows-wrap-and-turn-or-wt/

DIRECTIONS

Edging

With larger needle, CO 194 (206, 218, 234, 250, 274, 302, 342, 366) sts. Place beginning of rnd marker and join to work in the rnd, being careful not to twist sts.

For sizes 32.75 (34.75, 36.75)" only:
Work 1x1 Rib pat over 52 (58, 64) sts, K1, PM, (P1, K4, P1, K1, P1, K6, P1, K1) twice, PM, work Garter st over 12 sts, PM, (K1, P1, K6, P1, K1, P1, K4, P1) twice, PM, work 1x1 Rib pat over 52 (58, 64) sts, K1, PM, work Garter st for 12 sts. Work even for 3 rnds.

For sizes 40 (42.75, 46.75, 51.25)" only:
Work 1x1 Rib pat over 56 (64, 70, 84) sts, K1, PM, (P1, K2, P1, K1, P1, K4, P1, K1, P1, K6, P1, K1) twice, PM, work Garter st over 18 (18, 24, 24) sts, PM, (K1, P1, K6, P1, K1, P1, K4, P1, K1, P1, K2, P1) twice, PM, work 1x1 Rib pat over 56 (64, 70, 84) sts, K1, PM, work Garter st for 18 (18, 24, 24) sts. Work even for 3 rnds.

For sizes 55.75 (59.75)" only:
Work 1x1 Rib pat over 76 (88) sts, K1, PM, (P1, K2, P1, K1, P1, K4, P1, K1, P1, K6, P1, K1, P1, K8, P1, K1) twice, PM, work Garter st over 30 sts, PM, (K1, P1, K8, P1, K1, P1, K6, P1, K1, P1, K4, P1, K1, P1, K2, P1) twice, PM, work 1x1 Rib pat over 76 (88) sts, K1, PM, work Garter st for 30 sts. Work even for 3 rnds.

Body

Please choose the correct charts according to size. Charts A, B, and C are for the front and Charts D, E, and F are for the back.

For sizes 32.75 (34.75, 36.75)" only: K to M, SM, work Chart A twice, SM, continue Garter st, SM, work Chart D twice, SM, K to M, continue Garter st to end.

For sizes 40 (42.75, 46.75, 51.25)" only: K to M, SM, work Chart B twice, SM, continue Garter st, SM, work Chart E twice, SM, K to M, continue Garter st to end.

For sizes 55.75 (59.75)" only: K to M, SM, work Chart C twice, SM, continue Garter st, SM, work Chart F twice, SM, K to M, continue Garter st to end.

For all sizes: Continue Garter, charted, and St st pat as established until piece measures 15", ending with an odd rnd of the charted pat.

Dividing

*Work to M, remove marker, work to M, SM, P3, BO 6 (6, 6, 12, 12, 18, 18, 24, 24) sts, P3, SM; rep from * once more. 182 (194, 206, 210, 226, 238, 266, 294, 318) sts. Cut yarn.
Transfer the first 91 (97, 103, 105, 113, 119, 133, 147, 159) sts for front to holder. 91 (97, 103, 105, 113, 119, 133, 147, 159) sts remaining for back. For the back, the lace pat is on the right as worn.

Back

Join yarn to remaining sts on the RS, ready to work back and forth.
Next 2 Rows: Sl 1, K2, SM, work to last 3 sts, SM, K3.
Work in pat until piece measures 1.5 (1.5, 1.5, 2, 2, 2, 2.5, 2.5, 2.5)" from armhole, ending after a WS row.

Note: Inc Row can be worked on the RS or WS.
Next Row, Inc Row (RS or WS): Sl 1, K to M, M1, SM, work to M, SM, M1, K to end. 2 sts inc. Rep Inc Row every 6 (7, 7, 6, 7, 7, 7, 7, 8)th row 5 more times. 103 (109, 115, 117, 125, 131, 145, 159, 171) sts. 9 Garter sts at each armhole edge.

Work in pat until piece measures 5.75 (6, 6.25, 6, 6.5, 6.75, 7, 7.5, 8)" from armhole, ending after a WS row.

Cap Sleeve Shaping

Note: Right and left cap sleeve shaping occur at the same time, followed by the back neck BO.

Short Row 1 (RS): Sl 1, work to last M, SM, K7, W&T.
Short Row 2 (WS): Work to last M, SM, K7, W&T.
Short Row 3: Work to 1 st before wrapped st in previous row RS row, W&T.
Short Row 4: Work to 1 st before wrapped st in previous row WS row, W&T.
Rep last 2 rows 2 (2, 2, 4, 4, 4, 4, 4) more times.

Neck Shaping

Next Row (RS): Work to M, SM, work 18 (21, 24, 25, 27, 29, 36, 43, 48) sts, drop yarn and place these sts on holder for Right Shoulder. Join second ball of yarn, BO 49 (49, 49, 49, 53, 55, 55, 55, 57) sts. 27 (30, 33, 34, 36, 38, 45, 52, 57) sts remaining on LH needle for Left Shoulder.

Left Shoulder Shaping

Short Row 1 (RS): K16 (20, 24, 24, 24, 28, 36, 40, 48), W&T.
Short Row 2 (WS): Purl.
Short Row 3: K12 (15, 18, 18, 18, 21, 27, 30, 36), W&T.
Short Row 4: Purl.
Short Row 5: K8 (10, 12, 12, 12, 14, 18, 20, 24), W&T.
Short Row 6: Purl.
Next Row (RS): K to end, knitting wraps together with its wrapped st as you come to them.
Next Row (WS): Sl 1, K to M, remove M, P to end. Cut yarn, leaving a 36" tail for seaming. Place sts on holder.

Right Shoulder Shaping

Transfer right shoulder sts to larger needle, ready to work on the WS. 27 (30, 33, 34, 36, 38, 45, 52, 57) sts.

Short Row 1 (WS): P2, work 14 (18, 22, 22, 22, 26, 34, 38, 46) sts, W&T.
Short Row 2 (RS): Work in pat to last 2 sts, K2.
Short Row 3: P2, work 10 (13, 16, 16, 16, 19, 25, 28, 34) sts, W&T.
Short Row 4: Rep Short Row 2.
Short Row 5: P2, work 6 (8, 10, 10, 10, 12, 16, 18, 22) sts, W&T.
Short Row 6: Rep Short Row 2.
Next Row (WS): P to M, remove M, K to end, working wraps together with its wrapped st as you come to them.
Cut yarn, leaving a 36" tail for seaming. Place sts on holder.

Front

Transfer 91 (97, 103, 105, 113, 119, 133, 147, 159) front sts to larger needle. Join yarn, ready to work on the RS.
Next 2 Rows: Sl 1, K2, SM, work to last 3 sts, SM, K3. Work in pat until piece measures 1.5 (1.5, 1.5, 2, 2, 2, 2.5, 2.5, 2.5)" from armhole, ending after a WS row.

Note: Inc Row can be worked on the RS or WS.
Next Row, Inc Row (RS or WS): Sl 1, K to M, M1, SM, work to M, SM, M1, K to end. 2 sts inc.
Rep Inc Row every 6 (7, 7, 6, 7, 7, 7, 7, 8)th row 5 more times. 103 (109, 115, 117, 125, 131, 145, 159, 171) sts.

Work in pat until piece measures 5.75 (6, 6.25, 6, 6.5, 6.75, 7, 7.5, 8)" from armhole, ending after a WS row.

Neck Shaping

Note: Cap sleeve shaping occurs after the Front Neck BO and worked separately for the right and left.

Next Row (RS): Sl 1, work in pat for 26 (29, 32, 33, 35, 37, 44, 51, 56) sts, drop yarn and place these sts on holder for Left Shoulder. Join second ball of yarn, BO 49 (49, 49, 49, 53, 55, 55, 55, 57) sts. 27 (30, 33, 34, 36, 38, 45, 52, 57) sts remaining on LH needle for Right Shoulder.

Right Cap Sleeve Shaping

Short Row 1 (RS): K2, work to last M, SM, K7, W&T.
Short Row 2 (WS): Work in pat to end.
Short Row 3: K2, work to 1 st before wrapped st in previous row RS row, W&T.
Short Row 4: Rep Short Row 2.
Rep last two rows 2 (2, 2, 4, 4, 4, 4, 4, 4) more times, ending after a WS row.

Right Shoulder Shaping

Short Row 1 (RS): K2, work 14 (18, 22, 22, 22, 26, 34, 38, 46) sts, W&T.
Short Row 2 (WS): Work in pat to last 2 sts, P2.
Short Row 3: K2, work 10 (13, 16, 16, 16, 19, 25, 28, 34) sts, W&T.
Short Row 4: Rep Short Row 2.
Short Row 5: K2, work 6 (8, 10, 10, 10, 12, 16, 18, 22) sts, W&T.
Short Row 6: Rep Short Row 2.
Next Row (RS): K to end, knitting wraps together with its wrapped st as you come to them.
Next Row (WS): K to M, remove marker, P to end. Cut yarn, leaving 36" tail for seaming. Place sts on holder.

Left Shoulder Shaping

Transfer Left Shoulder sts to larger needle, ready to work on the WS. 27 (30, 33, 34, 36, 38, 45, 52, 57) sts.

Left Cap Sleeve Shaping

Next Row: Short Row 1 (WS): P last M, SM, K7, W&T.
Short Row 2 (RS): Knit.
Short Row 3: Work to 1 st before wrapped st in previous row WS row, W&T.
Short Row 4: Rep Short Row 2.
Rep last two rows 2 (2, 2, 4, 4, 4, 4, 4, 4) more times, ending after a RS row.

Next Row: Short Row 1 (WS): P16 (20, 24, 24, 24, 28, 36, 40, 48), W&T.
Short Row 2 (RS): Knit.
Short Row 3: P12 (15, 18, 18, 18, 21, 27, 30, 36), W&T.
Short Row 4: Knit.
Short Row 5: P8 (10, 12, 12, 12, 14, 18, 20, 24), W&T.
Short Row 6: Knit.
Next Row (WS): P to M, remove marker, K to end, working wraps together with its wrapped st as you come to them.

Cut yarn, leaving a 36" tail for seaming. Place sts on holder.

Finishing

Transfer shoulder sts to needle. With RS facing, seam each shoulder with 3-Needle BO.

With smaller needle, starting from the right side of Back Neck BO, PU and K 45 (45, 45, 45, 49, 51, 51, 51, 53) sts from Back Neck BO, 6 sts from Back Left Shoulder, 14 (14, 14, 17, 17, 17, 20, 20, 20) sts from Front Left Shoulder, 45 (45, 45, 45, 49, 51, 51, 51, 53) sts from Front Neck BO 14 (14, 14, 17, 17, 17, 20, 20, 20) sts from Front Right Shoulder, 6 sts from Back Right Shoulder. Place beginning of rnd marker. 130 (130, 130, 136, 144, 148, 154, 154, 158) sts.

Rnd 1: Knit.
Rnd 2: *K1, P1, rep from * to end.
Rep Rnds 1-2 once. BO loosely in knit.

Weave in ends and block to measurements.

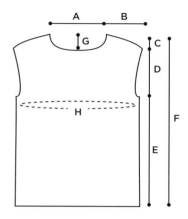

A 8.25 (8.25, 8.25, 8.25, .75, 9.25, 9.25, 9.25, 9.5)"
B 4.5 (5, 5.5, 5.75, 6, 6.25, 7.5, 8.75, 9.5)"
C 1"
D 6.75 (7, 7.25, 7.5, 8, 8.25, 8.5, 9, 9.5)"
E 15"
F 22.75 (23, 23.25, 23.5, 24, 24.25, 24.5, 25, 25.5)"
G 2 (2, 2, 2.5, 2.5, 2.5, 2.5, 2.5, 2.5)"
H 32.75 (34.75, 36.75, 40, 42.75, 51.25, 55.75, 59.75)"

Legend

knit
RS: knit stitch
WS: purl stitch

purl
RS: purl stitch
WS: knit stitch

yo
yarn over

k2tog
Knit two stitches together as one stitch

ssk
Slip one stitch as if to knit, slip another stitch as if to knit. Insert left-hand needle into front of these 2 stitches and knit them together

Chart A

Row	16	15	14	13	12	11	10	9	8	7	6	5	4	3	2	1
4		●							●		●					●
3		●	O	/	O	/	O	/	●		●	O	/	O	/	●
2		●							●		●					●
1		●	\	O	\	O	\	O	●		●	\	O	\	O	●

Chart B

Row	21	20	19	18	17	16	15	14	13	12	11	10	9	8	7	6	5	4	3	2	1
4		●							●		●					●		●			●
3		●	O	/	O	/	O	/	●		●	O	/	O	/	●		●	O	/	●
2		●							●		●					●		●			●
1		●	\	O	\	O	\	O	●		●	\	O	\	O	●		●	\	O	●

Chart C

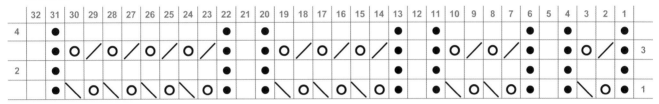

Row	32	31	30	29	28	27	26	25	24	23	22	21	20	19	18	17	16	15	14	13	12	11	10	9	8	7	6	5	4	3	2	1
4		●									●		●							●		●					●		●			●
3		●	O	/	O	/	O	/	O	/	●		●	O	/	O	/	O	/	●		●	O	/	O	/	●		●	O	/	●
2		●									●		●							●		●					●		●			●
1		●	\	O	\	O	\	O	\	O	●		●	\	O	\	O	\	O	●		●	\	O	\	O	●		●	\	O	●

Chart D

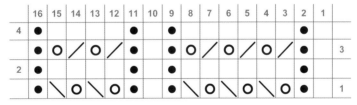

Row	16	15	14	13	12	11	10	9	8	7	6	5	4	3	2	1
4	●					●		●							●	
3	●	O	/	O	/	●		●	O	/	O	/	O	/	●	
2	●					●		●							●	
1	●	\	O	\	O	●		●	\	O	\	O	\	O	●	

Chart E

Row	21	20	19	18	17	16	15	14	13	12	11	10	9	8	7	6	5	4	3	2	1
4	●			●		●					●		●							●	
3	●	O	/	●		●	O	/	O	/	●		●	O	/	O	/	O	/	●	
2	●			●		●					●		●							●	
1	●	\	O	●		●	\	O	\	O	●		●	\	O	\	O	\	O	●	

Chart F

Row	32	31	30	29	28	27	26	25	24	23	22	21	20	19	18	17	16	15	14	13	12	11	10	9	8	7	6	5	4	3	2	1
4	●			●		●					●		●							●		●									●	
3	●	O	/	●		●	O	/	O	/	●		●	O	/	O	/	O	/	●		●	O	/	O	/	O	/	O	/	●	
2	●			●		●					●		●							●		●									●	
1	●	\	O	●		●	\	O	\	O	●		●	\	O	\	O	\	O	●		●	\	O	\	O	\	O	\	O	●	

LENOX SHAWL

by Tian Connaughton

FINISHED MEASUREMENTS

About 58" long at lower edge, 46" at upper edge, 16" deep

YARN

Knit Picks Stroll Tonal Sock Yarn (75% Superwash Merino Wool, 25% Nylon; 462 yards/100g): Shale 26753, 1 skein.

NEEDLES

US 6 (4mm) 32" circular needles, or size to obtain gauge.
US 8 (5mm) 32" circular needles, or size two sizes larger than used to obtain gauge.

NOTIONS

Yarn Needle
Stitch Markers
Cable Needle

GAUGE

20 sts and 36 rows = 4" in St st on smaller needles, blocked.

Lenox Shawl

Notes:

Lenox is a crescent shaped shawl worked from the bottom up beginning with the larger needles for the lace edging. Change to smaller needles to work the body of the shawl. The lace edging flows into the stockinette with an easy mesh transition. Short rows are worked in the stockinette section to shape the shawl. The shawl has 3 sts of Garter Stitch at each end, which is maintained throughout. Work RS chart rows (odd numbers) from right to left, and WS rows (even numbers) from left to right.

5-st RC: Sl 3 sts on CN and hold to back, K2, K3 from CN.
4-st LC: Sl 2 sts on CN and hold to front, K2, K2 from CN.
4-st RC: Sl 2 sts on CN and hold to back, K2, K2 from CN.

Lace Pattern (worked flat over multiples of 16 sts plus 7)
Row 1: K3, *P1, YO, K2tog, P2, YO, K2, K3tog, K2, YO, P2, K2tog, YO; rep from * to last 4 sts, P1, K3.
Row 2: K4, *P2, K2, P7, K2, P2, K1; rep from * to last 3 sts, K3.
Row 3: K3, *P1, K1, YO, K2tog, P2, 5-st RC, P2, K2tog, YO, K1; rep from * to last 4 sts, P1, K3.
Row 4: K4, *P3, K2, P5, K2, P3, K1; rep from * to last 3 sts, K3.
Row 5: K3,*P1, K2, YO, K2tog, P1, K5, P1, K2tog, YO, K2; rep from * to last 4 sts, P1, K3.
Row 6: K4, *P4, K1, P5, K1, P4, K1; rep from * to last 3 sts, K3.
Row 7: K3, *P1, K3, YO, K2tog, K5, K2tog, YO, K3; rep from * to last 4 sts, P1, K3.
Row 8: K4, *P15, K1; rep from * to last 3 sts, K3.
Row 9: K3, *P1, K4, YO, K2tog, K3, K2tog, YO, K4; rep from * to last 4 sts, P1, K3.
Row 10: K4, *P15, K1; rep from * to last 3 sts, K3.
Row 11: K3, *P1, 4-st RC, P1, YO, K2tog, K1, K2tog, YO, P1, 4-st LC; rep from * to last 4 sts, P1, K3.
Row 12: K4, *P4, K1, P5, K1, P4, K1; rep from * to last 3 sts, K3.
Row 13: K3, *P1, YO, K2, SSK, P2, YO, K3tog, YO, P2, K2tog, K2, YO; rep from * to last 4 sts, P1, K3.
Row 14: K4, *P4, K2, P3, K2, P4, K1; rep from * to last 3 sts, K3.
Row 15: K3, *P2, YO, K2, SSK, P1, P2tog, YO, P2, K2tog, K2, YO, P1; rep from * to last 4 sts, P1, K3.
Row 16: K4, *K1, P4, K2, P1, K2, P4, K2; rep from * to last 3 sts, K3.
Row 17: K3, *P3, YO, K2, SSK, P3, K2tog, K2, YO, K2; rep from * to last 4 sts, P1, K3.
Row 18: K4, *K2, (P4, K3) twice; rep from * to last 3 sts, K3.
Row 19: K3, *P4, YO, K2, SSK, P1, K2tog, K2, YO, P3; rep from * to last 4 sts, P1, K3.
Row 20: K4, *K3, P4, K1, P4, K4; rep from * to last 3 sts, K3.
Row 21: K3, *P1, K2tog, P2, K2, K3tog, K2, P2, K2tog; rep from * to last 4 sts, P1, K3. 92 sts dec.
Row 22: K4, *P1, K2, P5, K2, P1, K1; rep from * to last 3 sts, K3.

DIRECTIONS

With larger needle, loosely CO 375 sts. Do not join.
Rows 1-3: Knit.
Rows 4-25: Work one repeat of Lace Pattern, using written instruction or chart – 283 sts remain.
Change to smaller needle.
Row 26 (RS): K3, *K2tog, YO; rep from * across to last 4 sts, K4.

Row 27 (WS): K3, P across to last 3 sts, K3.
Row 28: K3, *K1, YO, Sl1, K2tog, PSSO, YO; rep from * across to last 4 sts, K4.
Row 29: K3, P across to last 3 sts, K3.
Rows 30-33: Rep Rows 26-27 twice more.

Begin Short-row Shaping
Short-row 1 (RS): K148, turn.
Short-row 2 (WS): P13, turn.
Short-row 3: K12, SSK, K4, turn – 282 sts remain.
Short-row 4: P16, P2tog, P4, turn – 281 sts remain.
Short-row 5: K20, SSK, K4, turn – 280 sts remain.
Short-row 6: P24, P2tog, P4, turn – 279 sts remain.
Continue to work short-rows as established (working to 1 st before gap, SSK or P2tog, work next 4 sts, turn) for 48 more rows, ending with a WS row – 231 sts remain.
Next Row (RS): K across to gap, SSK, K across to end of row – 230 sts remain.
Next Row (WS): K3, P across to gap, P2tog, P to last 3 sts, K3 – 229 sts remain.
Next Row: Knit.
BO Row (WS): *P2tog, return st to left hand needle; rep from * to end. All stitches bound off.

Finishing

Weave in all ends. Block to measurements, pinning points.

Lenox Chart

Column headers (left to right): 23 22 21 20 19 18 17 16 15 14 13 12 11 10 9 8 7 6 5 4 3 2 1

Row numbers (right side, odd) / (left side, even): 22, 21, 20, 19, 18, 17, 16, 15, 14, 13, 12, 11, 10, 9, 8, 7, 6, 5, 4, 3, 2, 1

Legend

knit
RS: knit stitch
WS: purl stitch

purl
RS: purl stitch
WS: knit stitch

yo
RS: Yarn Over
WS: Yarn Over

k2tog
RS: Knit two stitches together as one stitch
WS: Purl 2 stitches together

k3tog
RS: Knit three stitches together as one
WS: Purl three stitches together as one

c3 over 2 right
RS: sl2 to CN, hold in back. k3, then k2 from CN

c2 over 2 right
RS: sl2 to CN, hold in back. k2, k2 from CN

c2 over 2 left
RS: sl 2 to CN, hold in front. k2, k2 from CN

ssk
RS: Slip one stitch as if to knit, Slip another stitch as if to knit. Insert left-hand needle into front of these 2 stitches and knit them together

WS: Purl two stitches together in back loops, inserting needle from the left, behind and into the backs of the 2nd & 1st stitches in that order

p2tog
RS: Purl 2 stitches together
WS: Knit 2 stitches together

no stitch
Placeholder - no stitch made.

pattern repeat

ALIZE

by Amanda Schwabe

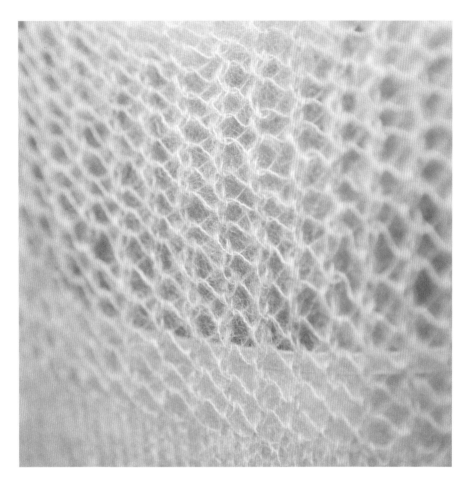

FINISHED MEASUREMENTS

42.5 (46, 50, 53.5, 58.5, 62, 66, 69.5, 74.5)" finished bust measurement; garment is meant to be worn with 12" of positive ease.

YARN

Knit Picks Aloft (75% Super Kid Mohair, 25% Silk; 246 yards/25g): Blush 25205, 4 (5, 5, 6, 6, 7, 7, 8, 8) balls

NEEDLES

US 7 (4.5mm) straight or circular needles, or size to obtain gauge
US 5 (3.75mm) straight or circular needles, or two sizes smaller than size used to obtain gauge

NOTIONS

Yarn Needle
Stitch Markers, including 2 removable

GAUGE

18 sts and 30 rows = 4" in St st on larger needles, blocked.
18 sts and 30 rows = 4" in Ridge Lace Pattern on smaller needles, blocked.

Alize

Notes:

This tunic-length pullover is knit in a lace-weight yarn at a worsted-weight gauge. It's knit in pieces from the bottom up and then seamed together and features drop shoulders, a roomy neckline, and a very over-sized fit. It will look perfect over a camisole, t-shirt, tank top, long-sleeved t-shirt, dress, skinny jeans... you get the idea. Try layering this light and airy piece over every outfit in your wardrobe.

The garment pictured was knitted with the Ridged Lace pattern, but if you're not into knitting lace, you can substitute Seed Stitch (see below) for all the Ridged Lace sections. Work the Seed Stitch on the larger-sized needles and ignore the instructions that tell you to switch needle sizes.

Unless otherwise indicated, slip all sts P-wise. The chart is followed from right to left on RS rows (odd numbers) and left to right on WS rows (even numbers).

Stockinette Stitch (St st, worked flat over any number of sts)
Row 1 (RS): K.
Row 2 (WS): P.
Rep Rows 1-2 for pattern.

Ridged Lace (worked flat over a multiple of 2 sts)
Row 1 (RS): K1, *YO, K2TOG TBL; rep from * to last st, K1.
Row 2 (WS): P1, *YO, P2TOG; rep from * to last st, P1.
Rep Rows 1-2 for pattern.

Seed Stitch (worked flat over a multiple of 2 sts)
Row 1 (RS): *K1, P1; rep from * to end.
Row 2 (WS): *P1, K1; rep from * to end.
Rep Rows 1-2 for pattern.

K1, P1 Ribbing (worked flat over a multiple of 2 sts plus 1)
Row 1 (RS): *K1, P1; rep from * to last st, K1.
Row 2 (WS): *P1, K1; rep from * to last st, P1.
Rep Rows 1-2 for pattern.

K2TOGFB: K2tog but don't slide the sts off the LH needle, then K2tog TBL into those same sts and slide to the RH needle.

Mattress Stitch
Sew the running sts to each other, one full st in from each edge. A tutorial can be found at: http://tutorials.knitpicks.com/wptutorials/mattress-stitch/

DIRECTIONS

Front
Using smaller needles, CO 98 (106, 114, 122, 134, 142, 150, 158, 170) sts.

Work in Ridged Lace pattern until piece measures 4.5" from beginning, ending after a WS row.

Switch to larger needles and work in St st until piece measures 20.5 (21, 21.5, 22, 22.5, 23, 23.5, 23.5)" from beginning, ending after a WS row.

Switch to smaller needles and work in Ridged Lace pattern until piece measures 22 (22.5, 23, 23.5, 24, 24.5, 25, 25, 25)" from beginning, ending after a WS row.

Shape Neckline
Set up for Neck (RS): Without working across the row, count 37 (41, 45, 49, 55, 59, 63, 67, 73) sts, PM, count 24 sts, PM, count 37 (41, 45, 49, 55, 59, 63, 67, 73) sts. Markers are now in place on either side of center neck sts.

Ridged-Lace Version Only
Next RS Row: Work in pattern until 2 sts before 1st M, K2TOGFB, remove 1st M, K1, pass the newly created st over, BO loosely to 2nd M, remove M, K2tog TBL, pass the previous st over, work in pattern to end. 38 (42, 46, 50, 56, 60, 64, 68, 74) sts rem on each side of BO sts.

Right Shoulder
Next and Following WS Neckline Shaping Rows: Work in pattern as established until 1 st remains at neck edge, Sl 1.
Dec Row 1 (RS): Sl 2, PSSO, BO 1, K2tog TBL, PSSO, work in pattern as established (beginning with a YO) to end. 4 sts dec.
Dec Row 2 (RS): Sl 2, PSSO, BO 1, work in pattern as established (beginning with a YO) to end. 2 sts dec.
Repeat Dec Row 2 twice more.
Dec Row 3 (RS): Sl 1, K2TOG TBL, PSSO, work in pattern as established (beginning with a YO) to end. 2 sts dec. 26 (30, 34, 38, 44, 48, 52, 56, 62) sts.

Work even in pattern until piece measures 5" from bottom of neckline, ending after a RS row.
Last Row (WS): Purl.
BO all sts K-wise.

Seed Stitch Version Only
Next RS Row: Work in pattern until 1 st before 1st M, KFB, remove M, K1, pass the newly-created st over, BO in pattern to 2nd M, remove M, BO 1, work in pattern to end.
Next and Following WS Neckline Shaping Rows: Work in pattern as established until 1 st remains at neck edge, Sl 1.
Dec Row 1 (RS): Sl 2, PSSO, BO 2, work in pattern as established to end. 3 sts dec.
Dec Row 2 (RS): Sl 2, PSSO, BO 1, work in pattern as established to end. 2 sts dec.
Repeat Dec Row 2 twice more.
Dec Row 3 (RS): Sl 2, PSSO, work in pattern as established to end. 1 st dec.
Repeat Dec Row 3 once more. 26 (30, 34, 38, 44, 48, 52, 56, 62) sts remain.

Work even until piece measures 5" from bottom of Neckline, ending after a WS row.
BO all sts K-wise.

Left Shoulder
Ridged Lace Version Only
Join yarn at Neckline Edge, leaving a 6" tail, and work one WS row even in established pattern, beginning with a P2TOG and omitting the initial P1.

Next and Following RS Neckline Shaping Rows: Work in pattern as established until 1 st remains at neck edge, Sl 1.

Dec Row 1 (WS): Sl 2, PSSO, BO 1, P2TOG, psso, work in pattern as established (beginning with a YO) to end. 4 sts dec.

Dec Row 2 (WS): Sl 2, PSSO, BO 1, work in pattern as established (beginning with a YO) to end. 2 sts dec.

Repeat Dec Row 2 twice more.

Dec Row 3 (WS): Sl 1, P2TOG, PSSO, work shoulder as established to end. 2 sts dec. 26 (30, 34, 38, 44, 48, 52, 56, 62) sts.

Next RS Row: Resume working Ridged Lace pattern.

Work even in pattern until piece measures 5" from bottom of Neckline, ending after a RS row.

Last WS Row: Purl.

BO all sts K-wise.

Seed Stitch Version Only

Join yarn at Neckline Edge, leaving a 6" tail, and work one WS row even in established pattern.

Next and Following RS Neckline Shaping Rows: Work in pattern as established until 1 st remains at neck edge, Sl 1.

Dec Row 1 (WS): Sl 2, PSSO, BO 2, work in pattern as established to end. 3 sts dec.

Dec Row 2 (WS): Sl 2, PSSO, BO 1, work in pattern as established to end. 2 sts dec.

Repeat Dec Row 2 twice more.

Dec Row 3 (WS): Sl 2, PSSO, work in pattern as established to end. 1 st dec.

Repeat Dec Row 3 once more. 26 (30, 34, 38, 44, 48, 52, 56, 62) sts remain.

Work even until piece measures 5" from bottom of Neckline, ending after a WS row.

BO all sts K-wise.

Back

Using smaller needles, CO 98 (106, 114, 122, 134, 142, 150, 158, 170) sts.

Work in Ridged Lace pattern until piece measures 4.5" from beginning, ending after a WS row.

Switch to larger needles and work in St st until piece measures 25 (25.5, 26, 26.5, 27, 27.5, 28, 28, 28)" from beginning, ending after a WS row.

Switch to smaller needles and work in Ridged Lace pattern until piece measures 30 (30.5, 31, 31.5, 32, 32.5, 33, 33, 33)" from beginning, ending after a WS row.

Shape Neckline

Set up for Neck (RS): Without working across the row, count 29 (33, 37, 41, 47, 51, 55, 59, 65) sts, PM, count 40 sts, PM, count 29 (33, 37, 41, 47, 51, 55, 59, 65) sts. Markers are now in place on either side of center neck sts.

Left Shoulder

Ridged-Lace Version Only

Next RS Row: Work in pattern until 2 sts before 1st M, K2TOGFB, remove 1st M, K1, pass the newly-created st over, BO loosely to 2nd M, remove M, K2TOG TBL, pass the previous st over, work in pattern to end. 32 (36, 40, 44, 50, 54, 58, 62, 68) sts remain on each side of BO sts.

Next and Following WS Neckline Shaping Rows: Work in pattern as established until 1 st remains at neck edge, Sl 1.

Dec Row (RS): Sl 1, K2TOG TBL, PSSO, work in pattern as established (beginning with a YO) to end. 2 sts dec.

Work Dec Row 2 times more. 26 (30, 34, 38, 44, 48, 52, 56, 62) sts remain.

Next WS Row: Purl.

BO all sts K-wise.

Seed Stitch Version Only

Next RS Row: Work in pattern until 1 st before 1st M, KFB, remove 1st M, K1, pass the newly-created st over, BO loosely to 2nd M, remove M, K1, pass the previous st over, work in pattern to end.

Next and Following WS Neckline Shaping Rows: Work in pattern as established until 1 st remains at neck edge, Sl 1.

Dec Row (RS): Sl 2, PSSO, work in pattern as established to end. 1 st dec.

Work Dec Row 2 times more. 26 (30, 34, 38, 44, 48, 52, 56, 62) sts remain.

Next WS Row: Work in pattern.

BO all sts K-wise.

Right Shoulder

Join yarn at Neckline edge, leaving a 6" tail. Work one row (WS) in pattern, beginning with a P2TOG instead of a P1 for the Ridged Lace.

Ridged-Lace Version Only

Next and Following RS Neckline Shaping Rows: Work in pattern as established until 1 st remains at neck edge, Sl 1.

Dec Row (WS): Sl 2, PSSO, work in pattern as established (beginning with a YO) to end. 1 st dec.

Work Dec Row 2 times more. 26 (30, 34, 38, 44, 48, 52, 56, 62) sts remain.

Next RS Row: Knit.

BO all sts P-wise.

Seed Stitch Version Only

Next and Following RS Neckline Shaping Rows: Work in pattern as established until 1 st remains at neck edge, Sl 1.

Dec Row (RS): Sl 2, PSSO, work in pattern as established to end. 1 st dec.

Work Dec Row 2 times more. 26 (30, 34, 38, 44, 48, 52, 56, 62) sts remain.

Next RS Row: Work in pattern.

BO all sts P-wise.

Sleeves (make 2 the same)

The sleeves are worked flat from the wrists up.

Using smaller needle, CO 31 (33, 33, 37, 39, 41, 43, 45, 45) sts. Work in K1, P1 Ribbing until piece measures 4.5" from beginning, ending after a WS row.

Switch to larger needles and work in St st, increasing 2 sts every 8 (8, 8, 6, 4, 4, 4, 4)th row 7 (6, 9, 11, 15, 17, 17, 20, 21) times as follows: K1, M1L, K to last st, M1R, K1. 45 (45, 51, 59, 69, 75, 77, 85, 87) sts.

Work even until sleeve measures 16 (16.25, 16, 15.5, 15, 14.25, 13.5, 15.25, 15.75)" or desired length from CO edge. BO all sts.

Finishing

Weave in ends. Wash and block to diagram. Allow to dry completely.

Use Mattress Stitch to sew all the sweater seams. Sew shoulder seams.

Sew in sleeves, centering the BO edge at the shoulder seam. Sew sleeve seams.

Sew side seams, starting 9 (8.5, 8.25, 8.25, 8.5, 8.5, 8.5, 8.25)" up from the CO edge measured on the front piece.

Weave in remaining ends.

Chart A

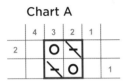

Legend

knit
RS: knit stitch
WS: purl stitch

○ yo
yarn over

↘ k2tog tbl
RS: Knit two stitches together in back loops as one
WS: Purl two stitches together as one

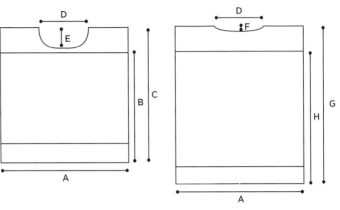

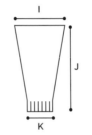

A 21 (23, 25, 27, 29, 31, 33, 35, 37)"
B 22 (22.5, 23, 23.5, 24, 24.5, 25, 25, 25)"
C 27 (27.5, 28, 28.5, 29, 29.5, 30, 30, 30)"
D 10"
E 5"
F 1.5"
G 30 (30.5, 31, 31.5, 32, 32.5, 33, 33, 33)"
H 25 (25.5, 26, 26.5, 27, 27.5, 28, 28, 28)"
I 9.75 (10, 11, 13, 15, 16.25, 16.75, 18.5, 19.25)"
J 16 (16.25, 16, 15.5, 15, 14.25, 13.5, 15.25, 15.75)"
K 6.25 (6.75, 7, 7.75, 8.25, 8.75, 9.25, 9.5, 9.5)"

Abbreviations							
BO	bind off	M	marker		stitch	TBL	through back loop
cn	cable needle	M1	make one stitch	RH	right hand	TFL	through front loop
CC	contrast color	M1L	make one left-leaning	rnd(s)	round(s)	tog	together
CDD	Centered double dec		stitch	RS	right side	W&T	wrap & turn (see
CO	cast on	M1R	make one right-lean-	Sk	skip		specific instructions
cont	continue		ing stitch	Sk2p	sl 1, k2tog, pass		in pattern)
dec	decrease(es)	MC	main color		slipped stitch over	WE	work even
DPN(s)	double pointed	P	purl		k2tog: 2 sts dec	WS	wrong side
	needle(s)	P2tog	purl 2 sts together	SKP	sl, k, psso: 1 st dec	WYIB	with yarn in back
EOR	every other row	PM	place marker	SL	slip	WYIF	with yarn in front
inc	increase	PFB	purl into the front and	SM	slip marker	YO	yarn over
K	knit		back of stitch	SSK	sl, sl, k these 2 sts tog		
K2tog	knit two sts together	PSSO	pass slipped stitch	SSP	sl, sl, p these 2 sts tog		
KFB	knit into the front and		over		tbl		
	back of stitch	PU	pick up	SSSK	sl, sl, sl, k these 3 sts		
K-wise	knitwise	P-wise	purlwise		tog		
LH	left hand	rep	repeat	St st	stockinette stitch		
		Rev St st	reverse stockinette	sts	stitch(es)		

Knit Picks yarn is both luxe and affordable—a seeming contradiction trounced! But it's not just about the pretty colors; we also care deeply about fiber quality and fair labor practices, leaving you with a gorgeously reliable product you'll turn to time and time again.

THIS COLLECTION FEATURES

Lindy Chain
Fingering Weight
70% Linen, 30% Pima Cotton

Comfy Sport
Sport Weight
75% Pima Cotton, 25% Acrylic

Alpaca Cloud
Lace Weight
100% Baby Alpaca

Galileo
Sport Weight
50% Merino Wool, 50% Viscose from Bamboo

Shimmer
Fingering Weight
70% Baby Alpaca, 30% Silk

Hawthorne Kettle
Fingering Weight
80% Superwash Fine Highland Wool, 20% Polyamide

Stroll Glimmer
Fingering Weight
70% Fine Superwash Merino Wool, 25% Nylon, 5% Stellina

Shine Sport
Sport Weight
60% Pima Cotton, 40% Modal

Aloft
Lace Weight
75% Super Kid Mohair, 25% Silk

Stroll
Fingering Weight
75% Superwash Merino Wool, 25% Nylon

Stroll Tonal
Fingering Weight
75% Superwash Merino Wool, 25% Nylon

View these beautiful yarns and
more at www.KnitPicks.com